▶▶▶▶▶▶▶ Cinema One

6 Alain Resnais, or the Theme of Time

Alain Resnais, or the Theme of Time

John Ward

London

Secker & Warburg in association with the
British Film Institute

The Cinema One Series is published by
Martin Secker & Warburg Limited
14 Carlisle Street, London W1
in association with *Sight and Sound*
and the Education Department of the
British Film Institute, 81 Dean Street London W1

General Editors
Penelope Houston and Tom Milne (*Sight and Sound*)
Peter Wollen (Education Department)

Alain Resnais, or the Theme of Time by John Ward
first published by Martin Secker & Warburg 1968
is a *Sight and Sound* publication
Copyright © John Ward 1968

S B N 436 09867 9 (hardcover)
436 09858 X (paperback)

Designed by Farrell/Wade

Printed in Great Britain by
Jarrold and Sons Limited, Norwich

Contents

Cover: Delphine Seyrig in *Muriel*. Photograph by Liliane de Kermadec.

Sources

Henri Bergson was a prolific writer, but I have been able to confine my exposition and quotation of his thought, in so far as it relates to the present study, to two of his more important books. The main source for this or indeed any account of Bergson's work is his *Time and Free Will*, translated by F. L. Pogson (fourth edition, Allen and Unwin, 1921). And to develop my analysis of Resnais' treatment of memory, I have also quoted from Bergson's *Matter and Memory*, translated by N. M. Paul and W. Scott Palmer (Allen and Unwin, 1918).

In the case of the films themselves, I have used the published scripts of *Hiroshima Mon Amour* translated by Richard Seaver (Grove Press, 1961) and of *L'Année Dernière à Marienbad* translated by R. Howard (John Calder, 1962).   J.W.

Toute la Mémoire du Monde, Resnais on the roof of the Bibliothèque Nationale; and (*below*) during the making of *Hiroshima Mon Amour*

Introduction

'How horrible is man's condition! He does not own one happiness whose source does not lie in ignorance of some kind.' *Balzac.*

Alain Resnais is not an original thinker, yet from heterogeneous sources he has produced a series of highly idiosyncratic films which are not just stylistically similar, but have a thematic continuity not always apparent in the scripts on which they are based. The framework within which this act of synthesis is made possible is the philosophy of Henri Bergson, augmented by an almost Proustian obsession with associationism. In view of the theoretical bias of his work, an excursion into philosophy is an unavoidable prelude to an analysis of Resnais' themes.

The Philosophy of Henri Bergson

Bergson tries to provide his philosophy of 'mental consciousness' with the appearance of scientific rigour by drawing it from a rather esoteric consideration of the nature of such concepts as 'space', 'time', 'number', 'motion', 'multiplicity' and so on. This strategy, however, cannot hide the basically anti-rational and literary quality of his thought, which proceeds more often than not by means of analogies.

Essentially he wanted to defend human freedom, threatened by the theory of evolution which exalted the influence of environment, and by current theories of psycho-physical parallelism. A consideration of Zeno's paradoxes taught him that, if one uses intellect to analyse processes such as motion, the only result could be confused notions of inevitability. The peculiar function of the intellect appears to be to separate into parts what should be continuous, and more particularly to isolate phenomena in space. Mathematics, the supreme and most typical creation of intelligence, consists of the manipulation through addition, subtraction and so on, of parts, numbers and fractions, never of processes. And number is something we could only conceive by spatialising objects. From this and similar considerations, Bergson came to the conclusion that intellect, which inevitably functioned in a spatial mode, was capable merely of dealing with bits and pieces, and that if it came across a process continuous in time it would proceed to spatialise and so fragment that process.

For example, when we first hear a piece of music we tend to listen to each note or group of notes separately and so fragment it that the effects the composer intended are lost. According to Bergson, when we do this we treat the music as something which is almost extended in space. We lay the notes out one alongside the other as if they had no apparent organic relation to each other. We seem to listen so closely that we distinguish the parts of the composition without ever grasping it in its entirety. Thinking is substituted for hearing, and we apprehend the music as analogous to a number of physical objects which must be isolated and intellectually conceived through a partly spatial medium.

The object of intelligence is *matter*, and intelligence treats everything as though it were a material object. Matter is extended in space and it restricts and drags everything downwards into inertia. Perhaps it is even created by intellect (Bergson is close to Berkeley here), the faculty which is the source of all man's psychological and social problems, precisely because it fragments his emotional life, separates his past, present and future, and by treating him as a physical object convinces him that he is not free.

Opposed to matter is *life*, the vital force, which surges upwards to break free of matter, as a continuous process of becoming in time. Life, which is beyond the scope of intellect, becomes free by organising matter to its purposes as an artist manipulates his materials. This is achieved by *intuition*, which operates within time and apprehends the world not as separate fragments but as continuity. Only through intuition can we grasp the essential wholeness of our lives and realise that we are free. So to return to the musical analogy: when we become familiar with a composition we are able to respond to it as a living form which has internal unity and develops within the temporal mode. 'We recall the notes of a tune, melting, so to speak, into one another. Might it not be said that, even if the notes succeed one another, yet we perceive them in one another, and that their totality may be compared to a living being whose parts, although distinct, permeate one another just because they are so closely connected.' (*Time and Free Will*, p. 100.)

Only gradually do we overcome the domination of intellect and learn to intuit the composition of our own lives as organic wholes. So by intuition we can reduce the physical world to a purely human significance; but when intuition is dominated by intellect, the physical world escapes from its subordinate context within the lives of men and presses in on them, as it presses in on Sartre's Roquentin and on the narrator of *Marienbad*. Only when we intuit our lives in time do we become free.

This account seems to make intuition inevitable, for how can we approach our pasts, presents and futures other than through the medium of time? All too easily, in fact: we can spatialise our lives in exactly the same way that we can spatialise the notes of a piece of music. Bergson distinguishes between two kinds of time. There is clock time which is conceived of as a series of discrete, homogeneous points which are one-directional. This is time on a spatial model: the time of intellect, '*mauvaise foi*' and Heidegger's 'forfeiture'. Distinct from this is pure or heterogeneous time which is multi-directional, and in which past, present and future time are fused and continuous. This is time of intuition; and paradigmatically the chronology of our mental lives which has been so thoroughly explored in literature from Joyce to the practitioners of *le nouveau roman*.

Through the mode of pure time, intuition creates (or perceives) the essence of life which is *duration*, the basis of self identity. 'Pure duration is the form which our conscious states assume when our ego lets itself live, when it refrains from separating its present state from its former states.' (*Time and Free Will*, p. 100.) Since it is to be found in heterogeneous time, duration is 'a succession of *qualitative* changes which melt into and permeate one another, without precise outlines' (p. 104). Duration, then, is that state in which our present and our past are one: in which our lives are a continuous stream of becoming and never something made or finished. We intuit the duration of our lives in their wholeness as we appreciate a piece of music in its entirety, and as we have to *learn* to appreciate music so we have to learn to perceive the durational quality of our lives. We are so habituated to the intellectual approach, which makes time homogeneous, that it is with the utmost difficulty that we can see things in any other way than in bits and pieces.

Duration exhibits itself most perfectly through the faculty of *real memory*. Physically we live through a series of instants that are unique and distinct from each other. Without memory we should have no past, only a series of presents which changed before we were even aware of them. Living through a memory-less life would be like watching a film running through so quickly that it was a kind of subliminal blur. Memory is essential to knowledge, understanding, feeling and sensation: in fact, to all that we mean by consciousness.

Bergson distinguishes between two types of memory. *Motor mechanism* or *mémoire volontaire*—in which remembering something means simply being able to repeat it (e.g. chunks of poetry). It is habit pure and simple, which can be invoked by the intellect or the will for practical purposes. There need be no memory of previous occasions on which we learned these chunks of poetry, or indeed any consciousness of the past involved in it at all. *Pure memory*, independent recollections or *mémoire involontaire*—here the past is remembered imaginatively and re-created (as with, say, Proust's *petite madeleine*). There is no habit or reflex involved.

This is a mental process and not merely a mechanism in the brain.*

Through involuntary memory, the past is brought into the present and the passage of clock time is suspended in an awareness of the duration of inner psychological time. 'With pure memory the totality of our past is continually pressing forward so as to insert the largest possible part of itself into the present action' (*Matter and Memory*). Certainly in Resnais' films the past forces itself into the present, but because the memory processes of his characters are not pure, though certainly they are in some ways unsolicited, the past goes through a rigorous vetting before it is allowed in. As we shall see later, the memories of the hero and heroine of his first two films are only apparently involuntary.† In fact they are dictated by reason because the two characters have fragmented their pasts to such an extent that only their obsessive recollections are revived. The past as a whole is unremembered.

When these two kinds of memory cohere, when pure memory directs habit memory and when habit memory provides data for pure memory to work on, our lives will have duration. 'The characteristic of the man of action is the promptitude with which he summons to the help of a given situation all the memories which have reference to it' (*Matter and Memory*, p. 198). So 'in memory the past lives on into the present and interpenetrates it. Apart from mind the world would be perpetually dying and being born again; the past would have no reality and therefore there would be no past. It is memory, with its correlative desire, that makes the past and the future real and therefore creates true duration and true time' (Russell, *History of Western Philosophy*). Through memory, intuition re-creates the past and infuses it into the present and we are able to grasp the flow of our lives. The

---

* The distinction between voluntary and involuntary memory is the basis of Bergson's influence on Proust, even though the novelist denies it.

† In *Hiroshima Mon Amour*, for instance, the girl's memory of Hiroshima is a motor mechanism. It does not involve conscious re-creation of the past as her memory of Nevers does. Thus 'you know nothing of Hiroshima' but 'you are Nevers'.

Filming the lunch-party sequence in *Muriel*. Photograph by Liliane de Kermadec →

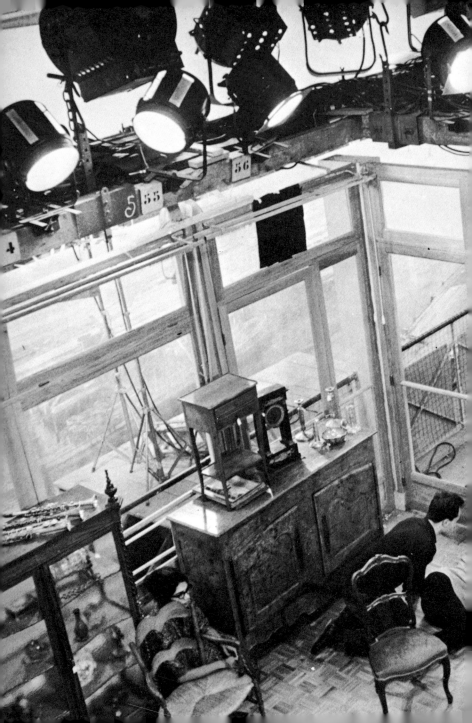

essence of life for Bergson is change, the durational flux of the vital spirit, which among all the characters of Resnais' films, only Diego in *La Guerre est Finie* makes any progress towards grasping. The creative energy of life demands that we *act*, in accordance with our whole experience, and determine our own change, our own evolution. But we can do this only when we have subdued intellect and intuited the process of becoming which is ourselves. When we have done this, we shall see that evolution can be creative, and that we are free. At this point Bergson lapses into silence, and the way is open for future thinkers such as Sartre to define more precisely what it is to 'act authentically'.

The aesthetic implications of this philosophy are dealt with more fully in the chapter on Resnais and his sources. Here it is sufficient to note that Bergson compares the activity of intuition with that of the artist re-creating his experiences in his art. Indeed, pure memory which is 'perfect from the outset' alone has aesthetic value because it forms the raw material of art. So Proust can conclude that only in art do we discover true reality. From similar premises Proust developed a new aesthetic, and Resnais elaborates the existential dilemma of man. Proust urges us to live through art; Resnais contemplates the difficulties of living in time, with the past hovering over us when we want to forget and receding into the shadows when we need to remember. Time is destroying us (*déjà!*) as it destroys empires and civilisations.

So we arrive at the Bergson–Proust dichotomy of Time the destroyer and Memory the preserver. But, as Bergson points out and as Resnais never tires of affirming, memory does more than preserve; it also creates. The individual apprehends the universe as an aggregate of images (cf. Robbe-Grillet), one of which is his body around which all the rest are centred. When we perceive the world certain images are made to stand out from an 'indifferent background'. These explicit images isolated from memory (i.e. pure memory) are *pure perceptions*. When these specific images are placed within the past images of *pure memory* which are preserved whole and intact, they become *concrete perceptions* which

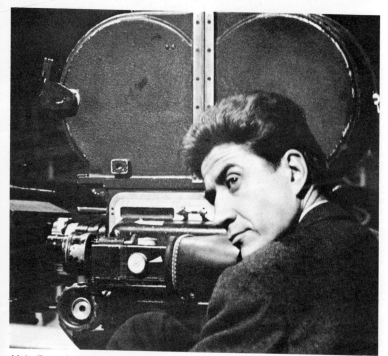
Alain Resnais, photograph by Agnès Varda

are subsequently structured and significant. Thus the equation is: pure perceptions (impersonal specific images) + pure memory (clusters of whole past images) = concrete perceptions (personally significant images—subjective). Thus through memory *the* world becomes *my* world. We shall see how time and again this philosophical analysis is given artistic expression by Resnais, especially through the girl from Nevers.

It is this creative aspect of memory that provides problems for Resnais. If our present lives are forged by our memories ('the past impregnates the present'), this can give us a sense of duration, but might it not create certain difficulties? First of all, how can we be sure that our past is compatible with our present? Might not the impregnation of our present by our past make us aware of the *dis*continuity of the process of our becoming? Is Proust's conviction that involuntary memories of tastes and odours, 'rediscovered under entirely different circumstances,' evoke the past in its wholeness, anything more than a personal experience which works for him but might conceivably escape others? These are some of the questions implied in *Hiroshima Mon Amour*. Secondly, how can we be sure that our memory will serve us correctly? Might not our memory be forced to serve our desires and needs, even though—indeed because—it is involuntary? Might we remember the past not as it is, but as we would like it to be? In both Bergson and Proust the term 'involuntary' is treated synonymously with inviolate; but since Freud can we really believe, on trust, that any psychological function is free from the effects of what an organism needs or what its motives are? We require more evidence than Bergson and Proust give us to believe that something which is recalled unwillingly must be recalled accurately. These questions are implied by *L'Année Dernière à Marienbad*. If our memory deceives us about the past, and our memory of the past forges our present, then not only will our past be an illusion but our present also.

1: Hiroshima Mon Amour

Hiroshima Mon Amour is a difficult film because of its theme. What happens is quite clear, but the sense of these happenings is harder to define and arguably not deducible from the film alone. None of Resnais' feature films is entirely self-explanatory. We have to refer to a theoretical tradition to understand them fully. The tradition of Baudelaire and Nerval which culminates in Bergson and Proust.

In *Hiroshima* two lovers are drawn together by their memories and at the same time are separated by them. They both have a need to remember and yet also a need to forget. How is this possible?

Resnais appears to make a distinction between public and private memories which corresponds closely to Bergson's motor mechanism/independent recollection classification. Great events in which we were not personally involved are almost inevitably forgotten. With the passage of time we become so insensitive to other people's suffering that we can lie in the disused ovens of Auschwitz and have our photographs taken as souvenirs. Yet a personal slight will remain in our minds, constantly affecting our attitudes to those we feel have insulted us. And however hard we try to remember the agony of the Jews in Auschwitz or to forget a trivial insult, it seems to do no good. In an important sense, therefore, it is almost impossible for man to escape from his own egocentricity; and this is tragic, for it is vital that we do remember Auschwitz and that, in one way, we forget an insult.

The memory of Auschwitz should play a part in everyone's growth. It is, or should be, an inescapable fact of our lives. Without it we can have no duration, since we develop within a context of which the fact of Auschwitz is an integral part. It is part of us, and we are as responsible for it as we are for ourselves. We cannot think about it without asking ourselves, 'what has it contributed to me and what am I contributing to it?' Auschwitz did not end in 1945: it exists in what we all are.* So how can Cayrol refrain from bringing up the question of responsibility in *Nuit et Brouillard*?

On the other hand, a trivial insult must be forgotten as an *isolated* event and remembered as part of our life process. It is because we cut the insult off from the rest of our past that preceded and succeeded it that it assumes such magnified proportions. Isolate something and it will look much bigger than it does in context. And much more important too.

Let us take the example of two tragedies: the destruction of Hiroshima and the brutality at Nevers. The girl has only known Hiroshima as a public event. She has seen the city as a 'tourist', recording everything but 'understanding nothing'. She has seen the films, read the eye-witness accounts, thrilled with horror at the reconstructions in the museum, but she was not there when it happened. She has not conceived a deformed child, her parents were not incinerated by the explosion. To the Japanese who has experienced it personally (although he was not physically present, it was his city, his life, his parents and friends that were destroyed), she is an intruder into his tragedy. When she mentions that she has visited the museum, we see his impression of what the museum means to her. Flashing neon signs appear on the screen, honky tonk music on the soundtrack, as we hear her words and see the museum. To her it is nothing but a side-show, and no matter how hard she tries to 'feel' it will never be anything more. Empathy

---

* I don't find this kind of blame-sharing very attractive myself. It confuses issues. Blame everyone and you blame no one *in particular*. Only by analysing the social development that leads to fascism can we avoid it in future: i.e. use the intelligence that Bergson so dislikes.

is no substitute for experience. And he is equally distant from her experiences at Nevers. To him, at first, Nevers is 'a pretty French word' and he savours the beauty of her phrase 'jeune à Nevers'.

Yet if personal tragedies appear somewhat inaccessible to other people, they must be remembered by the victims because these experiences are an integral part of their lives. Without them (Hiroshima and Nevers), the man and the girl would not be what they are. But because these tragedies have been personally experienced they tend to be remembered as isolated events which overshadow everything else close to them in time. Since they made such an impact, the protagonists find it difficult to fit them into the stream of things; to give them a context. There does not seem to be any context large enough. But this is so only because they intellectualise the experiences. This may seem a strange thing to say about something that plays primarily on the emotions, but when something has a great emotional effect we tend to analyse it a great deal (see the next chapter on *Marienbad*). If we are to appreciate our lives in their continuity, however, we need to forget traumatic experiences as isolated events and remember them within the general context of our development. Moreover, this need to forget is increased by the obvious desire to rid ourselves of a painful memory. As a result, there is a continual conflict between two opposing needs.

In the case of other people's tragedies, as we have seen, the difficulty is in remembering. Our knowledge is by description and not by acquaintance. But there is a way in which we can become virtually acquainted with such a tragedy even though it has ceased physically to exist. This is by experiencing the memory of it through its effect on someone we love. And it is this route to acquaintance that provides the problems of the protagonists in *Hiroshima*. Without it they would be two people eternally separated by their own memories; with it they are both drawn to and separated from each other. 'You are killing me, you make me feel wonderful' has more than a sexual connotation for the girl.

Even lovers rarely acquire this route to acquaintance, because the attitude that an individual usually has to his personal tragedies

From the opening sequence of *Hiroshima Mon Amour* (*frame enlargements*) →

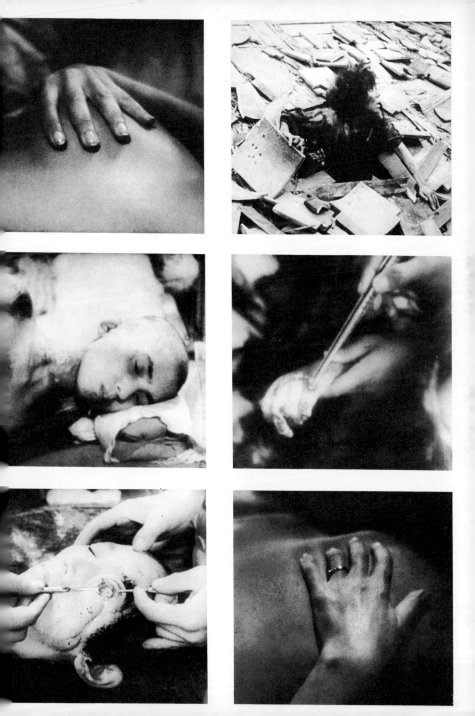

is prohibitive. He tends to regard them as his own private property. It is, for example, galling to someone who has been through the concentration camps to be told by someone who has not that he understands it or can imagine what it was like. There are some things that we feel no one has any right to talk about unless he has personally experienced them. An outsider should be humble before the facts. This attitude tends to separate people. Even lovers remain apart to some extent because of their experience; and if this experience is traumatic, then their separation is likely to develop into conflict. This makes a satisfactory and lasting love relationship difficult, but there are two special characteristics of love affairs that make the task of achieving a mutual sense of duration even more complex.

Lovers have a compulsive desire to confide in or hear confidences from each other. For example, the Japanese needs to learn about Nevers and feel that he knows something about the girl that she has never told anyone, especially her husband. He is closer to a more profound truth than he realises when he says 'Because of Nevers I can only begin to know you.' But he does not realise that such knowledge will involve him in conflict with her, while her husband's ignorance makes his relationship with her less turbulent. The more the Japanese presses her to reveal herself, the more she will resent his intrusion upon her past. Also, lovers need to attain some kind of shared identity, to lose or find themselves in each other ('devour me' etc.). This demand for mutual identity entails achieving some kind of mutual sense of duration which can only follow from personal revelation.

The Japanese wants to hear about Nevers because 'I feel that it was there that you begin to be what you still are today,' but she is reluctant to confide. The memory is painful and it belongs to her, not to him. Yet also, at first, she does not confide because on a conscious level she has forgotten. She admits this very early in the film. 'I had the *illusion* that one never forgets—even in love.' And even when she realises that her past is relevant to her present experiences in Hiroshima ('Why deny the obvious need to remember?'), she is aware that she cannot re-create the past by a

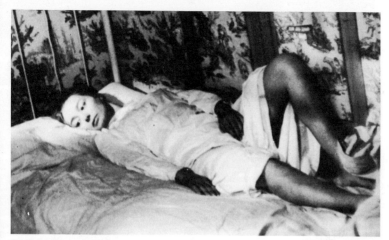

In the cellar at Nevers: Emmanuèle Riva

conscious effort: 'Like you I have forgotten.' When she does remember, the memory is involuntary (i.e. *mémoire involontaire*), evoked by the inevitable similarities between her love affairs with the German and the Japanese. And the memory of Nevers is painful because she has isolated it. She has not reconciled it with her life before and after it. But her love for the Japanese demands that she confide in him, and when she does she begins to see its relationship to him and its place in her whole life. Her dead German lover becomes associated with her live Japanese lover, and lives on in him.*

Yet she resists this process, and not simply because it causes her pain. As she re-creates the events at Nevers they both realise that she is what she is because of Nevers, and that this is something he cannot become part of unless she relaxes her hold on the

---

* Late in the film she says, 'Nevers, I would like to see you again.' Earlier she could never have said this. But now her old love has begun to relive in her anew, and now that Nevers is beginning to assume its place in her life instead of dominating it, she wants to see it to complete the change, to exorcise the pain of her memories and to face her past.

memory of her dead lover. He asks her 'Am I dead when you are in the cellar?' And she replies, 'You are dead!' If her present is to become pregnant with her past, her dead lover will cease to have an *independent* existence. He will become part of her present love affair. She will no longer be able to escape into the past and seek refuge with the German. This is almost impossible for her to accept because she is so used to living in the past: indeed, her life stopped at Nevers.* How can she therefore become willing to live completely in the present as her present love and lover demand? Yet by falling in love with the Japanese she has made an irrevocable step towards doing just that. It is impossible for her not to be reminded by him of her dead lover. Indeed she associates—even confuses—the two. We see her talking directly to the Japanese as she tells him that since her imprisonment in the cellar 'I have loved blood' and that 'I tasted your blood.' She addresses the Japanese but she is talking about the German whose head she cradled as he died. Resnais uses this technique frequently during her narrative. On several occasions when she speaks of Nevers to the Japanese she is to some extent speaking to the German.† The past is forcing itself into the present through these associations. Nevers is ceasing to be an isolated memory. Her dilemma, then, is caused by the gulf between her failure to go the whole way in impregnating her past into her present and her failure to prevent

---

* She admits this is self-indulgence: 'Like you I too have tried with all my might not to forget . . . Like you I wanted to have an inconsolable memory, a memory of shadows and stone' (text, p. 23). And Bergson analyses it: 'But he who lives in the past for the mere pleasure of living there and in whom recollections emerge into the light of consciousness without any advantage for the present situation, is hardly better fitted for action' (*Matter and Memory*, p. 198).

† Another example is a scene in the café when she describes the cellar. She speaks to the Japanese and says 'I remember only your name.' This can only refer to the German. Resnais thus emphasises the associations in her mind. At the end of the narrative, as we see her leaving Nevers on a bicycle at night, Resnais has on the soundtrack Japanese music from the café in which she describes the scene to her Japanese lover. Here again, past and present are impressionistically merged.

at least some of her past from forcing its way into her consciousness.

When she was a young girl in love with a German soldier, she lived instinctively in the pure Bergsonian sense. After the tragedy of Nevers she began to live the life of intellect. She ceased to have any sense of identity or continuity beyond these isolated events. She became dominated by certain physical memories and her existence was frozen in time. When she met and fell in love with the Japanese it was inevitable that her existence could no longer remain fixed at Nevers. She was bound to come alive again and instinct was bound to some extent to reassert itself. As a result she is torn apart by the conflict between instinct and intellect, between duration and discontinuity. She tries to escape from this conflict (i.e. from him), but it is too late, it has already begun. How will it all end? Who knows?

The situation of the Japanese is less complicated but not formally weaker. On a formal level she must be more complex than he in order to balance the disproportion between her tragedy (Nevers) and his, which is of universal significance. He feels separated from her because of her lack of personal acquaintance with Hiroshima, the central experience of his life. But, unlike her, he does not intellectualise this experience. It is part of his present life (after all, he lives in Hiroshima whereas she is unable to live in Nevers), but there is no suggestion that it has the crippling effect on him that Nevers has upon her. When he learns of her personal tragedy, he realises that she too has experienced something like the horror of his people. She is one of the few Westerners who could understand the impact of the bomb upon the Japanese. Others are perhaps the survivors of the concentration camps, the Burma Railway, Guernica, Dresden, the Warsaw ghetto and so on. He tries to understand what happened to her by comparing it to his own tragedy; by finding similarities. Significantly he asks her of Nevers, 'Does it rain sometimes?' Rain is his touchstone of danger, and to understand the agony she suffered in terms of the agony of Hiroshima, he immediately thinks of rain which brings down radioactive dust on his people. Human fear

The girl (Emmanuèle Riva) and the German soldier (Bernard Fresson)

has for him become associated with rain. Moreover, there are parallels which Resnais draws visually—the two rivers, the girl whose head is shaved and the women of Hiroshima whose hair falls out, the human skin of Hiroshima 'floating, surviving, still in the bloom of its agony' and the bleeding hands of Nevers ('They scrape. They rub the skin off . . .').

However, as he discovers, Nevers cuts her off from him in a way that Hiroshima never cuts him off from her. While he thinks that Hiroshima was a personal tragedy which can only be understood by those who have suffered similar tragedies, she guards her memories jealously. He is willing to share when he learns more about her, but she is not. Up to a point she is *made* to share, but she is never willing to do so. Quite late on in the film she declares 'How dare those who have never been to Bavaria talk about love.' Could any other remark so cruelly exclude the Japanese? Her attitude towards Nevers is, in fact, maladjusted; while his to

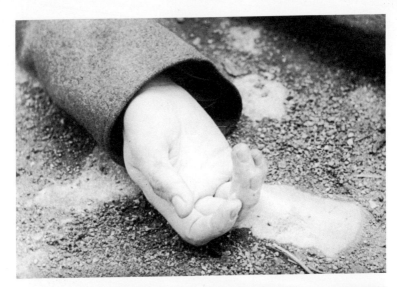

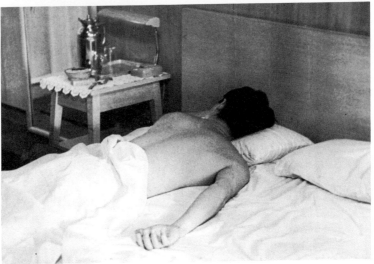

Hands at Nevers and Hiroshima

Hiroshima is not. Once he has discovered how deeply she has suffered, the context of Hiroshima can, for him, serve to unite them, because now it is a reminder of the similarity of their experience whereas once it constantly emphasised their separateness. But the knowledge that he has lived through events similar in their emotional effect to her own does not enable her to overcome the obstacle of Nevers. As far as he can tell, the dead lover claims her and part of her is seemingly lost to him for ever. He is not aware that she is reminded of the German by him and that a process (of recovery) has begun which could end in him, the Japanese, becoming her only love, in whom the German exists again. If only the Japanese knew about this there would be few problems for him, and what problems there were would not be insoluble.

She may be able to tell him about the events at Nevers, but she cannot tell him what is going through her mind as she does so. The evocation of the dead soldier by the position of the Japanese's hand, for example, is something he cannot know about even though she has told him of the soldier's death. At the time the significance of the association is something private to her. She is not just reminded of the German's death, but of a whole experience in its context of her life. This is involuntary memory as Proust understood it. Pure memory moves from a detail to a whole experience in an essentially private context, and so it is something that cannot be wholly communicated. This inhibits him from helping her to realise the triumph of her instinct over her intellect. And because she has not understood the significance of Hiroshima, as he has begun to grasp that of Nevers, she does not have the bridge that he has between her tragedy and his. In the last resort they cannot help each other, but neither can they leave each other. They have gone too far in sharing their pasts to leave, but they cannot go far enough to remain. They recognise that they belong to two different experiences, but they fail to realise that they have it within their power to achieve a mutual identity. Their separateness is neatly summed up in the café scene where they sit at different tables, unable to look at anyone but each other. There is no dialogue, only

Separate tables: Emmanuèle Riva and (*right*) Eiji Okada

the sound of water on the soundtrack. Water for him, the falling rain which is the dread of Hiroshima, and water for her, the Loire and its association with her past love affair. This apartness is again emphasised in the scene at the station when they sit on a bench next to an old Japanese woman. The girl is silent, alone with her thoughts, excluded from his talk with the old woman because it is in Japanese. The audience is made to feel her exclusion because this dialogue is not translated. Thus even in their obsession with each other, they are essentially apart. He cannot 'devour' her or 'deform' her in his own image, because personal memories always remain uniquely the possession of one person in some way or another.

As well as the impasse created by their failure to communicate, perhaps she is also prevented from accepting her affair with the Japanese completely *because* of its similarity with her previous affair. We have seen how these similarities extend her relationship with the Japanese, but in another part of her mind she might

Hiroshima railway station

associate the pleasure of love with death.* And because her relationship with the Japanese revives the details of her life with the German she is perhaps morbidly afraid that the Japanese too will (must?) die. So once again she cannot leave; she loves him and depends for her contact with her lost love upon him, but she cannot achieve a mature love relationship with him, because the last time she did it ended in death.

In spite of the fact that *Hiroshima Mon Amour* is obviously one of the great post-war films, I think Resnais has been led to exaggerate the nature of the girl's problems in order to make the film thematically consistent. The result is that *Hiroshima Mon Amour* is formally weaker than it might have been. By choosing to concentrate upon the experience of the girl, he has shifted the argument from the effects of personal memories on future relation-

---

* Certainly in the opening scene of the film, which is the only occasion on which we see them making love, Resnais himself equates love and destruction.

Emmanuèle Riva, Eiji Okada →

ships to a subject that is on the borderlines of abnormal psychology. The experiences of the girl were not of a kind that would give rise to normal personal memories, or even to the kind of memories which, just because of their extremeness, could serve as a paradigm of a class of 'standard' personal memories. Hers were in fact traumatic. It is not just her relationship with her Japanese lover that is affected: her whole life has been crippled. Hers (as it is shown in the film) is not a dilemma that allows talk about what she *should* do; it is one where it is appropriate to talk about what can be done *for* her. In other words, she is not a free agent. And certainly she is not typical or in any way representative of the kinds of personal problems normally experienced by normal people.

Resnais' difficulty springs from the fact that Marguerite Duras made the mistake of choosing to examine the wrong experience for his case. If she had concentrated on the more normal (i.e. in the sense of being non-traumatic) though by no means typical experience of the Japanese, the film would have gained a greater breadth of reference. There is no reason why the experience should be typical; indeed it is more likely to represent a whole class of somewhat heterogeneous events if it is not. The best way to represent such a class is to take an extreme example, on the grounds that if it works for the extreme case, it will work for the rest. This may be bad statistics but it is plausible art. It is essential, however, that the example chosen be a member of the given class. And in Resnais' case, the class is supposed to be of normal personal memories, not of abnormal ones as his example of the girl suggests.

Perhaps I will be accused here of setting up a theory, forcing the film to fit into it, and complaining when certain features of the script resist. Why should the girl's memories belong to a class of normal memories? Might not Duras *intend* her to be an emotional cripple? Hardly. To portray her as such would be to except her from all responsibility. We would no longer be able to talk about her making choices or having motives, in the full sense. She would be a person who could not participate in any very interesting way in a deep human relationship. She would not be an appropriate partner for the Japanese, psychologically or aesthetically, and it would not be legitimate to draw any very profound social, moral or emotional conclusions from a perusal of her. In other words, *Hiroshima* would be reduced to a rather trivial story whose theme was that a normal man and a psychotic woman are unlikely to develop a lasting love relationship. Indeed, to the extent that they achieve a deep relationship at all, the film would be false.

Ultimately, the impasse at which the lovers arrive is accounted for by the virtually psychotic nature of the girl's memories. In the preceding pages an explanatory model has been provided which accounts for this crippling effect of her past experiences. The advantages of this model are that it fits the facts and explains profundities in the film which would be lost if the psychotic role of the girl were to be accepted without qualification.

On this model, however, one must say that *Hiroshima* would have been a finer film had the psychotic element not been introduced. There is one more alternative: that the girl is not emotionally crippled at all. But she certainly does not behave as if she were adjusted to her experience. Anyway, what would a 'normal' response to the kind of experience she has suffered be like? Presumably it would be something like the adjustment made by the Japanese to Hiroshima, but continually we are shown that his attitudes are radically (qualitatively) different from hers. The simple fact is that, in various ways, she is not free to choose what she wants to do; and to that extent the film, as an analysis of how even lovers are kept apart by their pasts, is weakened. It is weakened because instead of developing the conflict between them, it assumes this conflict by making her the kind of woman any man would fail to get on with.

Yet there is a passage in the script which throws doubt on this interpretation and suggests that she is normal. Just one, but it must be disposed of. Several critics have noted that the girl from Nevers is happily married; and if she is in love with her husband, if she is capable of a full love relationship, it is hardly plausible to say that 'her life is fixed at Nevers' and that she is emotionally crippled. In this event, the problems of her affair with the Japanese

would be neither so extreme nor so novel. But what is the evidence for the contention that she is in love with her husband?

There is only one section in which her husband is mentioned, and it is longer in the published script than in the film:

SHE (*softly, as if in an aside*): What is your wife like?

HE (*purposefully*). Beautiful. I'm a man who's happy with his wife. (*Pause*)

SHE: So am I. I'm a woman who's happy with her husband. (*This exchange is charged with real emotion, which the ensuing moment covers*) (Script, p. 48.)

Neither of them mentions love, and the girl, by repeating almost word for word the man's phrase, responds automatically, tiredly, not with conviction. Indeed, the very phrase 'happy with her husband' suggests 'adapted to life with her husband' rather than 'in love with her husband'. Moreover, throughout the film she hardly behaves like someone who has a happy marriage. Would a happy wife say to another man 'Oh! How good it is to be with someone, sometime' (p. 68), as if this was one of the few times when she was close to anyone? Or would she admit 'I was hungry.

Hungry for infidelity, for adultery, for lies, hungry to die' (p. 74)?
And presumably, if she had a relationship with her husband which
involved mutual trust, she would think it important that he knew
about her affair with the German; but she says that he does not
know about it (p. 67). Nothing in the script supports the idea that
she is in love with her husband, and everything suggests that the
Japanese is the first man she is capable of loving since the German
died. And so the analysis of the girl stands, as someone who is
psychologically deformed.

So the question posed for Bergson (i.e. 'might not the impregnation of our present by our past make us aware of the *dis*continuity
of the process of our becoming') lacks point, since by making the
past event one that has a traumatic effect, a positive conclusion
has been assumed. Of course we shall lose all sense of duration
and order if the past experience we bring to the present has made
us more or less mentally unstable! Bergson could slide out of
this argument quite easily by saying that it is impossible for anyone
in such a state of mind ever to apprehend her past instinctively
anyway. But more likely he would point out that the experience

37

became traumatic in the first place because she insisted on fragmenting her past. Basically, no experience is unassimilable given an instinctive response. That the girl could not assimilate 'Nevers' points to something wrong even before her affair with the German soldier.

The success of *Hiroshima Mon Amour* is the success of an effective landscape (emotional), in which important and new configurations of objects are wrought. It is a success because it makes inspired connections, not because it makes a correct statement.

2: L'Année dernière à Marienbad

Marienbad is a difficult film because of its plot. Once we are clear about what exactly took place the year before and what is happening now, then we shall have solved most of the riddles of the film. The form and structure of the picture are of a memory working, and in order to analyse them we need to know exactly what the subject is; what the memory is working on.

A year ago a man X met a woman A at Marienbad in a château where they were both guests. Under the nose of her husband M, he began an affair with her. After trying several times to persuade A to leave with him, X is warned off by M. Finally M kills A and X is left alone to mourn.

The story is not told directly in the film, since the narrative follows the highly subjective re-creation of the past in the mind of X. The audience must read between X's wish fulfilments and rationalisations if it is to discover what really happened. But there are clues, as I shall try to show. We cannot even be certain that the three central characters appear as they really are. Indeed, it is quite likely that M was not the enigmatic, austere figure he is made to be. What we see is probably a reflection of X's feelings towards him, rather than an accurate picture of what M was really like.

When we remember the past, especially some tragedy in which we were involved, we don't simply reproduce what *actually* happened and sorrow over it. We tend to analyse the event; we postulate other possibilities: 'If only I'd done that she might have

left him and she'd be alive today.'* We multiply 'might have beens', we try to elucidate: 'Did she really mean that when she walked away?' 'Perhaps she was really encouraging me all the time. . . .' We try to shift or reassess blame; we suddenly notice something that suggests we might have been more understanding: 'I should have realised she was really afraid to come away with me when she . . . It wasn't that she didn't want to.' We notice warning signs, clues to the way things would eventually develop: 'I ought to have known he was dangerous by the way he . . .' Again and again we go over details of the past, following up various threads to the 'might have beens' that never were. The events themselves serve as a set of premises from which we construct arguments. Sometimes the past appears as inevitable; at other times we think we can see how things might have been different. Occasionally some detail will strike home as peculiarly significant (compare the film's use of overexposure). But the sum total of all these doubts and speculations is misery. We are only torturing ourselves by trying to alter something that is past and fixed.

The story of *Marienbad* is told (i.e. remembered) in this way by X. It is one long interior monologue.† A is dead, she does not narrate. When she appears to, it is simply X imagining or re-membering how she would or did speak.** At no point does she narrate. Mostly he describes a situation and we see her acting out his description. She conforms like a puppet to his account. At times when his version is contradicted by what we see on the screen (e.g. bedroom door, see p. 56) this is reality breaking through his fantasy. Moreover, the poses she adopts as he describes her are often so stagy that they cannot be the normal reactions of

---

* There is evidence in the film that at times X feels as responsible for A's death as M. Not that he murdered her but that he could have avoided the murder. The pistol gallery scenes represent both X and M's rivalry and a formalisation of A's death and their mutual responsibility for it.

† Resnais' and Robbe-Grillet's statements to the contrary are not relevant.

** 'Entities should not be multiplied without necessity.' X virtually admits that he is making events happen (i.e. in his mind) when he says 'Now you are here where I *brought* you,' etc.

Delphine Seyrig, Alain Resnais

'The poses she adopts are . . . the exaggerated attitudes she acquires in his fantasy'

a woman but the exaggerated attitudes she acquires in his fantasy. In terms of Bergson's thought, *analysing* the past is unfortunate. It is an example of memory at the service of intellect. In the place of a sense of duration, X breaks the past down into separate events and details of events. He fragments when he should connect. His affair with A, apprehended by instinct, would be a part of his becoming. He should not be concerned to alter the past since this would mean changing himself—which is anyway self-contradictory. All experiences, pleasant or painful, are grist to the mill. Growth, evolution and becoming are processes which continue irrespective of happiness if instinct is allowed to replace intelligence. But in X's case intelligence is in control; and since the object of intelligence is matter, X becomes dominated by physical objects. This, as we shall see later, is shown quite explicitly in the film.

Two drives meet rather conveniently in *Marienbad*. There is Robbe-Grillet's thesis (*chosisme*) that the only way to approach concepts is through physical objects and not, as most people would say, through consciousness. Consciousness for him is a highly suspect construction upon the sensible world. Memory and imagination are improbable devices that help us to live and satisfy our ego. They are legitimate as long as we realise that they are firmly dependent upon the physical, but men are egocentric and quickly assume that they are autonomous. So we have idealism sticking in our throats. What we need then is a Copernican revolution to bring about a return to the centrality of the physical as the only true reality.

Robbe-Grillet attempts this by analysing one of the most characteristically egocentric concepts, memory. Memory in which the existence of physical past depends upon the vagaries of the human mind. He shows that memory can only function validly in terms of a context of the continuous past. If the past is remembered in fragments, then confusion is inevitable. Memory depends for its validity upon an awareness of the duration of the physical world which is the basis of the duration of our emotional worlds. If this is absent, memory will lack a criterion and physical objects will be capable of several interpretations—each equally valid. So the physical will dominate: formless, discrete and ever present. So we have a neat jigsaw of two theses.

ROBBE-GRILLET	BERGSON
1. True reality = physical world	1. Intellect via memory fragments pasts
2. Memory leads to idealism if it becomes independent	2. Confusion—no duration
3. Idealism = confusion—no criterion of validity	3. Matter is object of intellect
4. Left with ubiquitous physical	4. Domination by matter

Robbe-Grillet's technique, as in all his novels, is a reflection and a demonstration of his thesis that the physical world is exclusively real. In all his work he defines character in terms of sense experience. At first glance there appears to be little development of character either in his novels or in *Marienbad*, but this is so because we expect direct psychological description. We are so used to the author intruding into a narrative to describe character or to show character that when such intrusions are absent we assume that character is also absent. Now, Robbe-Grillet lets character reveal itself not through behaviour or introspection, as is usual, but through perception.* The details of what a character sees (i.e. how the physical world appears to him), which depend upon the tendency of human beings to select certain features of their environment (pure perceptions) and ignore others, and to interpret those selected in terms of their own personal interest (concrete perceptions), reveal what the character is. In view of this, Robbe-Grillet seeks to trace the inner psychological world of his protagonists (nearly all of his writings are *about* a single character) as they register on objects. And *Marienbad* is no exception. Only one character, X, is revealed; and as usual

---

* There is a striking justification for this technique in Bergson: 'The formation of memory is never posterior to the formation of perception: it is contemporaneous with it' (Mind—Energy). Here Bergson asserts a necessary connection between the two faculties. It can be interpreted as a justification of Robbe-Grillet's attempt to analyse X's memory process (and character) in terms of his perceptions.

the medium of revelation is an environment of a past experience which is perceived again by him through memory. At the end of the film we should know a great deal about X. But we know little about M or A, and what we do know is not really about them but about what X thinks about them.

Notoriously Robbe-Grillet rejects interior monologue. Yet in a sense *Le Voyeur*, *Les Gommes* and *La Jalousie*, as well as *Marienbad*, can be said to be long interior monologues; but in a special sense, since the protagonists are not saying 'I am feeling, thinking etc. A.B.C.', but rather 'I am seeing A.B.C.' However, in Robbe-Grillet's view seeing reveals feeling, thinking etc.; indeed it stands in their stead, so that in his books and the film there is a monologue which is exterior and yet at the same time a revelation of the interior. And *Marienbad* is entirely in key with his novels, for what we learn about X's character comes not from what he does or thinks he does: anyone in a similar situation would behave (i.e. re-create the past) in the same way. His individuality comes through in his visual impressions, his images of the château, the corridors, the garden, A's gestures, the spatial positions of the guests in a room, and so on. For this reason *Marienbad*, unlike its predecessor, is a highly visual film.

Resnais is able to synthesise the Robbe-Grillet script with a Bergsonian outlook because Robbe-Grillet makes his narrative and thematic points through three central symbols which are as appropriate to Bergson's thought as to his own. The baroque hotel with its endless corridors and impersonal guests represents the confusion of the memory (or in Bergson's terms—memory/intellect) process. The 'frozen' guests in particular point to the way in which past events are fixed timelessly in personal recollection. The maze-like garden and complex ornamentation are extensions of this symbol.* How easy it is to get lost! Details proliferate, but any sense of overall design or form (i.e. duration) is absent. The fragmentation which Bergson abhors is the necessary

---

* 'Rooms heavily laden with decor from the past,' and 'that belongs to the past.' Again how well *Marienbad* is described by Bergson's phrase describing the psychological novelist as a 'painter of mental scenery.'

condition of the absence of a standard of memory reference that Robbe-Grillet predicates.

The second major symbol is the statue, which, in a sense, embraces the premises both of Robbe-Grillet and Bergson. Even a physical object is susceptible of several interpretations if we insist on intellectualising. Robbe-Grillet would say that we should accept the statue as something made known to our senses, and leave it at that. To search for meanings or explanations is to invite confusion. The physical world is its own explanation. Though, on an artistic level, the different ways in which X and A see the statue constitute Robbe-Grillet's basic technique of character revelation. But what is revealed here is the character not of two people but of one, X. If the reactions of X and A to the statue were to parallel their 'present' responses (i.e. his aggressive and hers cautious), then X would see the woman in the statue as having something revealed to her, while A would see her as being restrained; but in fact the reverse is true. This suggests that we do not observe A, but X's idea of A: A as he would like her to have been.

In a Bergsonian context the symbol of the statue would represent the isolated event: reality fragmented by the intellect. Of course, the statue is ambiguous deprived of a context, just as any event in a person's life is when cut off from what went before and came after it. But *in* this setting it would be explicit. Take a link from a chain and it can be many things. Leave it in the chain and it is only one: a link in a chain. This is the significance of a durational sense of one's past life.

Now it is by taking advantage of this kind of ambiguity, which derives from fragmenting the past, as re-created in memory, through the intellect, that X tries to persuade A (and himself) that they have met before as lovers. Apparently X used a rather trite line when he first approached A in the hotel. 'Haven't we met somewhere before?' And in his recollection of the previous year this question becomes very significant. If he wishes to persuade himself that A would have gone away with him if she had not been killed, then he will be able to make out a more plausible case if he can persuade himself that A believed his story of their previous

The statue in the garden

meeting. Indeed if he can persuade himself of this, then he can be certain of having triumphed over M.

In his memory/imagination he re-enacts how he might have gone more expertly about persuading her of this supposed meeting. To X the business of convincing 'her' of the truth of this prior meeting becomes synonymous with the business of persuading her to leave M and come away with him. The way he attempts this imaginary persuasion of her—and actual persuasion of himself—is by constantly appealing to isolated facts and objects, to the fragmented past. Cut off from their context in the continuous process of his life, they can be made to mean anything he wishes them to mean. And for Robbe-Grillet all such interpretations are illusions, so that any one of them is as 'valid' as any other. A photograph, the broken heel of a shoe, a smashed glass of wine and a negligée of feathers are offered as evidence. This is the exercise of intellect at its worst. Where in all this can there be any standard of reference? Once he begins searching for meanings in this way

The match game: Giorgio Albertazzi and Sacha Pitoëff

he soon gets to the stage where he can believe anything because there is no necessary connection between past events. He chews over several endings; the happy one in which they prepare to leave together before the real one of murder intrudes. He even imagines his own death by suicide or accident, presumably as some attempt to compensate for his own inadequacy. He imagines A being raped, and so on, but the more he imagines the more he suffers as a result. At one stage he reveals that he is arranging the past to suit himself, when he says, after the fact of her death has forced itself into his mind, 'No, this is not the proper ending: I need you alive.' The final 'happy' ending he constructs, in which they leave the hotel together, is significantly narrated in the past tense, as if to convince himself that it really did happen.

The third great symbol is the matchstick game, which crystal-lises the frustration of the lover who can never win (re-establish contact with reality through memory) and who cannot avoid the inevitable unhappy ending. Even by intellectual juggling, all his imaginings cannot change the past. The game has a mathematical

form which is Bergson's paradigm of intellectual operations. A eludes X in his memory because her only reality was in her physical presence, which exists no longer. She was lost to X when M murdered her and 'possessed' her ultimately. And no matter how many happy endings and evasions X imagines, he cannot change that. In the game M's triumph is constantly reaffirmed. The episodes of the game are moments when reminders of what actually happened break into X's thoughts.* As the husband

---

* This idea of the matchstick game as an image of reality can be developed further. At one moment, just after he has been alone with her, the scene of the game is flashed on the screen and he narrates 'Once again we were parted.' The fantasy in which they were alone and she was being persuaded by him is shattered as the image of the game breaks into his consciousness. Contrasted with it are the several scenes of them dancing together. Here he possesses her, they are together in one another's arms and for the moment what really happened has been forgotten. The dance scenes represent the moments in his 'remembering' when he has escaped from reality.

'The dance scenes represent the moments in his remembering when he has escaped from reality'

dominated the triangular relationship he will always win the game.

In another sense the game reinforces the notion of the randomness of a journey through memory. Once X begins to play he admits that he is 'making my way *at random* through the labyrinth.' He has not worked out a mathematical formula that will enable him to win every time: he just plays by ear. This symbolic similarity between the game and the hotel with its maze of corridors is again reinforced by the voice of the narrator saying 'And once again I walked down these same corridors, etc.' *as soon as* X picks up the first matchstick (see p. 55 of the script). There is no certainty in the game for X, just as there is no criterion of memory.

As X analyses and dissects the past more and more, he becomes hopelessly confused between appearance and reality and between past and present. And as he surrenders to his intellect, he loses all sense of duration and becomes lost in the physical. This is shown through A, who is the principal figure in his imaginings. Configurations of objects on her dressing-table and about her room

virtually leap at 'her' with his interpretation stamped upon them. Temporal sequence (i.e. the basis of duration) is destroyed by a series of rapid flashbacks in which the real and ideal are confused. Interpretations of the past become arbitrary in the midst of memories divorced from direct sensation and dominated by the ambiguity of physical objects.* X is trying to make objects fit the various interpretations he wishes to place upon the past, but

---

* 'And as the repeated picture of one identical objective phenomenon, ever recurring, cuts up our superficial psychic life into parts external to one another, the moments which are thus determined, determine in their turn, distinct segments in the dynamic and undivided progress of our more personal conscious states. Thus the mutual externality which material objects gain from their juxtaposition in homogeneous space reverberates and spreads into the depths of consciousness: little by little our sensations are distinguished from one another like the external causes which gave rise to them, and our feelings or ideas come to be separated like the sensations with which they are contemporaneous.' (*Time and Free Will*, p. 126).

53

The bedroom sequence: Delphine Seyrig →

because they are ambiguous he cannot force a single (false) reading upon them; the other (true) one keeps intervening.

The best example of this is the scene in A's bedroom (p. 123 of script). X's voice describes how she behaved, but on the screen we see that in fact this was not what she did. He has to admonish 'her' to jolt his memory back into fantasy. 'No, you weren't laughing' (film). 'And you turned back toward the bed . . . Oh, listen to me . . . Remember . . . Listen to me, please . . . Yes it's true.' And 'Where are you? Where have you gone? Why always try to escape?' (pp. 123–124 script). In the film he says, 'And you went back to the bed.' But she does not. Then later, when his memory is in check, he describes her as going to the bed four times, which she subsequently does. Why would there be this variation in the correctness of what he describes, if it were not that he was trying to deceive himself in the face of an unforgotten reality? A reality that is dreadful to contemplate: the death of his mistress. 'It was already too late. There was no more . . . The door was closed. No! No! The door was closed. Listen to me.' Obviously this means that the door was open and implies that someone whom X does not wish to remember came through. Robbe-Grillet affirms this when he writes the directions: 'And it is when she is quite close to the now open door that he speaks the last phrases, in a desperate struggle against the images seen on the screen. It is the bedroom door.' In the film this scene is introduced by X saying (of or to A) 'It's a question of your life.' In view of what follows this is quite explicit.

By manipulating objects in this way, X is bound to end up utterly confused. For Robbe-Grillet memories depend on objects, and if we try to reverse this process we must be battered into a kind of delirium by the constant presence of differing configurations of objects in varying contexts. Or in Bergsonian terms, if we try to manipulate objects (use intellect) we shall become the slaves of objects (intellect). In either case the result is the same, 'a considerable mass of added decoration encumbering all the space with a *stifling* but *realistic* flood of embellishment' (p. 135). In the course of the film we experience with him and his alter ego the perplexity he feels once he has given himself up to memory/intellect.

The happy ending he eventually makes up for himself is not the ending of the film. What has gone before will undoubtedly come again; this memory process will be repeated many times, since there can be no satisfaction for him until he faces her death as an event in the general pattern of his life. The ending of the film is ironic, even tragic. 'She' is, as he says, 'already getting lost, forever, in the calm night, alone with me.' Lost in the recesses of his mind. *Marienbad* examines in detail the kind of 'intellectual' life that is the starting point of *Hiroshima Mon Amour*. The remembering X undergoes is something that the girl from Nevers must have experienced many times.

In style *Marienbad* is finely appropriate to its context. The use of over-exposure, rapid cutting to break down the normal temporal order and to juxtapose related scenes and gestures, are obvious and quite literal representations of the activities of memory, particularly its associative functions. In this respect *Marienbad* is not very different from its predecessor. Consider, for example, the similarities of function of the position of the lover's hand in *Hiroshima* and the position of A's arm nestling in the hollow of her shoulder in *Marienbad*. Again in accordance with the working of memory, Resnais will slow down a scene and have it played in silence to create tension when it is particularly significant to X. A good example is the scene where A breaks the glass. Here M figures predominantly, and so is a threat to X's sense of success with A. At other times fragments of dialogue anticipate the action, while others are faded when irrelevant. This is just how memory works, stimulated by odd phrases from the past and blocked by others that are off the point or too near it to be bearable. As well as anticipating the action by their remarks, the nameless guests in the hotel also serve as a kind of Greek chorus by occasionally warning (implicitly) X. When one of them says that the weather the previous year can be checked, he sets a limitation on the range of X's self-deception. A criterion has been established in all X's imaginings.

The 'happy ending': A (Delphine Seyrig) waits for X

A significant piece of furniture in X's memory is the theatre poster of the 'House of Rosmer' which is seen on one of the walls of the château. Much, too much, has been made of this. In Robbe-Grillet's script a poster is mentioned, but not named, though he does suggest it could be a play by Marivaux. The Rosmer idea is Resnais' and although it neatly makes a point, it does not materially affect one's understanding of the film. Its function is purely one of emphasis. X has probably seen the play, it is part of his experience, and when he remembers A he naturally thinks about it because it is similar in many ways to his own story. *Rosmersholm* too is a story of persuasion: the persuasion of Rosmer by Rebecca to reject Christianity and accept the new 'progressive' ideas of Peter Morgan. Later, Rosmer tries, at first unsuccessfully, to persuade Rebecca to marry him, and (happy omen for X!) they are finally united, albeit only in death. Only death can content Rosmer who, like X, is plagued by doubt that the woman genuinely loves him. Even Ibsen's and Robbe-Grillet's symbolism serve similar

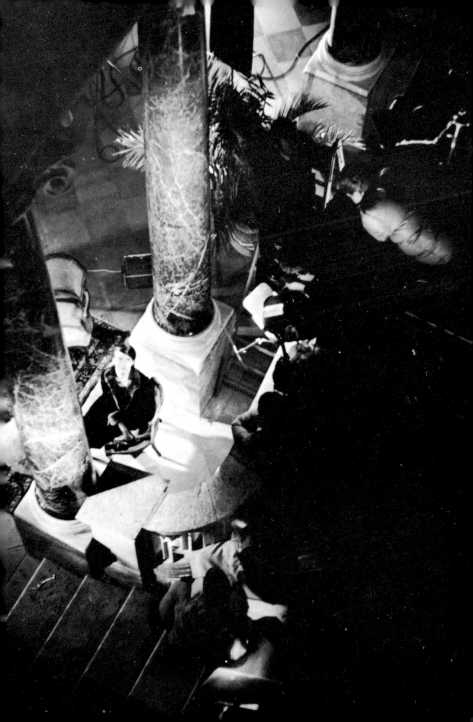

Giorgio Albertazzi, Delphine Seyrig

purposes: the Mill Stream and the Balustrade; the White Horses and the Match Game.

Robbe-Grillet's image of the poster has a much simpler function than Resnais gives it. In the script the poster provides some kind of justification for the play within the film. The play is used as a spur and a parallel to X's remembering. At times he confuses the actress with A and the play with his past experience. Significantly the play ends with the words 'I am yours,' but the actress does not move. This is a formalisation of X's desire and of his frustration.

Philosophically, *Marienbad* suffers from a central conceptual confusion which is specifically rejected by Bergson (see *Matter and Memory*, p. 173), along with associationism generally. It is assumed that the purpose of memory is somehow to recapture the past: that the relationship between the past and a recollection of it is similar to that between a model and a painting. The mind is

The play within the film: 'I am yours'

supposed to create pictures whose accuracy is to be tested by comparing them with the past they represent. Obviously, since we have not got the past at hand to provide a criterion, the only way we can compare these pictures with the past is by making further pictures of the past, and so on *ad infinitum*. Even if we compare our pictures of pictures with other people's (who have this past in common) pictures of pictures, we do not get any closer to the past. If we have the same pictures we might be making the same mistakes, and anyway psychological evidence shows that this kind of agreement is very rare. On this theory there is no real criterion of comparison.

The picture theory of memory is a necessary condition of associationism, which Resnais seems to accept wholesale and exclusively. However, most philosophers today would want to assimilate the memory process to the learning process. They would say that the way we know something has been learned (and remembered) is that the agent behaves or can behave (or talk) in certain ways. This approach seems to me more profitable and makes the theoretical implications of *Marienbad* largely irrelevant. Thus the question 'How can we be sure our memory serves us correctly?' cannot be answered positively on the picture theory, and on a more sophisticated theory it becomes a behavioural problem. 'How can we be sure X is behaving in certain kinds of ways?' We know that X remembers the past partly because he behaves as though he did.

As far as Resnais' view of memory is concerned, it would be useful to know how he would interpret Bergson's phrase 'refrains from separating its present state from its former state.' What else can memory do on the picture theory but separate these states? How can X do anything else but isolate his experience, on this view of memory?

3: Muriel

Muriel, in content, is the least complex of Resnais' feature films.*
Thematically it is also fairly straightforward, and its plot makes no
more demands on us than that of *Hiroshima*. Yet it is a difficult
film, perhaps the most difficult he has made. The reason for this
is Resnais' narrative technique, which relies to an extent rare in
the cinema on pure associationism. The confusions, jumps, non-
sequences of events that result are at first reminiscent of Benjy's
narrative in *The Sound and the Fury*; but in fact they are quite
different. Unlike the typical stream of consciousness novel, the
recital of *Muriel* is, in the main, strictly chronological. There are
flashbacks, but there is no attempt to dispense with conventional
time sequence altogether or to substitute for it the mental chronology of the characters. Indeed, compared to Benjy's meanderings
there is little difficulty about deciding which tense we are working
in.

So it would be mistaken to call *Muriel* a stream of consciousness film, since there is no interior monologue in it and no evidence
that the narrative is a reflection of the characters' sensations—
except on the few occasions when there are direct flashbacks, and

* The central characters of *Muriel* have affinities with the heroine of
Hiroshima and X of *Marienbad*. Where they have, I shall not reiterate
all the Bergsonian references but will just establish the resemblances,
assuming the reader can by now remember or work out the Bergsonian
points for himself.

even these seem to tell us less about the characters than about the director's intentions. In fact, if any consciousnesses are streamed they belong to Cayrol and Resnais and not to Hélène, Bernard and Alphonse. And so when I say that this is a film run through by associations, I mean the author's associations. Scenes are juxtaposed, seemingly trivial details are placed together, *apparently* for no other reason than that they are chronologically close. But normally in art irrelevances are omitted; and certainly in this film Resnais constantly enforces the principle of economy. Cuts from a meal being served to dirty dishes, after dinner attitudes from a cigar being lit to the stub being ground into an ashtray, and so on, suggest the passage of irrelevant time. So there are reasons why scenes are contrasted and the details in question are not trivial. Why, then, is it so difficult to discern what their significance is?

The answer has been stated above: the absence of narrative through character. One of the ways in which we understand what is going on in a book or film is by the way the characters develop and by what is going on inside them. In *Muriel* almost all this is absent, and we have to rely almost completely on plot to grasp the movement of the film. For motive, intention and purpose we have to look to situation, settings, objects and, in particular, other people. Cayrol's script, in common with the work of Robbe-Grillet, owes its technique to Husserl's phenomenology and, in particular, to the theory of intentionality.* The physical detail of appearance reveals character far more than dialogue.

Hélène's personality is revealed largely through her physical context. She is surrounded by the past (antiques) and she is living on borrowed time (sold dinner plates and the loans from Claudie). Bernard operates within a context of privacy and personal possessions (tape-recorders, cameras, notebooks). Alphonse is a man of

---

* Consciousness is characteristically consciousness of something, it points beyond itself. Consciousness is therefore revealed through its directedness to objects: its intentionality. And the physical world discloses its significance to us through the intentions we have towards it. Things have no intrinsic meaning. A hill, for instance, is only steep because we want to climb it.

Hélène (Delphine Seyrig) and Bernard (Jean-Baptiste Thierrée)

Characters in an environment: Hélène, Alphonse, Bernard and Françoise

shady deals and cafés. He is the one character who makes contact with people in the town. Françoise is chic but vulnerable. She appears self-assured, but she spends a lot of time alone for someone so attractive. The sight of Bernard on his white horse riding along the cliff-top, with its knightly associations, tells us more about his intentions and purposes than anything he says. The figure of justice on a white charger setting out to avenge wrongs, only to be confronted by a farmer asking about a mate for his goat, instead of by a damsel in distress, just about sums up Bernard's self-deception.

In these ways *Muriel* is more of a Robbe-Grillet film than *Marienbad*, and because interior monologue is absent and interaction between the characters is not explained by reference to their mental lives, what they do and say seems to be isolated as in *La Jalousie* and the rest of the novels. Moreover, cutting destroys most of our sense of character development. We feel that if, for once, we could get inside the characters, we might begin to work things out.

Bearing in mind the novelty of this largely present tense, highly objective film in the work of Resnais, what can we find in it which suggests it has a form and perhaps even some links with his previous work? When in doubt, begin with structure. There are two basic triangles of relationships in *Muriel*.

One is centred on Hélène, a middle-aged antique dealer and gambler whose former lover, Alphonse, returns to her after twenty years absence. They recall their past love affair and begin to disagree about who was responsible for its eventual breakdown. Alphonse appears as a thoroughly dishonest individual, who has run out on his wife after their restaurant business went bankrupt; who has picked up a young actress (Françoise) and quite cynically confronted Hélène with her; who continually tries to borrow money, and who undoubtedly treated Hélène shamefully twenty years before. His main concern seems to be to avoid responsibility and to exploit those around him for his own benefit, as he exploited the army and the war in Algeria through his café. All his talk of the war is distorted. He presents the old cliché about the army being a man's life, but we know that he did not see any action. Moreover, his café operated a colour bar against Arabs. Resnais indicates the extent of Alphonse's self-deception by having him say 'I was much better off in Italy,' when he was supposed to be in Algeria. He is by far the most repellent character in all of Resnais' films. He manipulates the past and its associations for others to suit himself. No wonder he says, 'I resent you, Hélène, for all those memories.' She reminds him of his dishonesty and his cheapness. And, of course, her memories represent a threat to his success in deceiving her in the present. He does not even have the excuse of an unpleasant experience to justify his distortions. Alphonse is one character who can be more richly described in existentialist (especially Sartrean) than in Bergsonian terms, because his personal failure springs from his lack of strength rather than from any misguided 'intellectual' approach to life.

He manages to persuade Hélène that he was really in love with her, mainly because she wants to believe him. She overlooks his obvious faults, and despite certain discrepancies in their recollections of the past, she accepts that it was something wonderful. Her wistfulness is destroyed by the arrival of the third member of the triangle, Alphonse's brother-in-law Ernest, who acts as a catalyst. He has come to Boulogne to force Alphonse to return to his sister. Hélène, who did not know that Alphonse's wife was still alive, is compelled to face up to his dishonesty. Finally Ernest reveals to her Alphonse's betrayal of her in the past. But she is unable to cope with the breakdown of her fantasy life, and runs away to the comfort of an old friend and her husband who look as though they belong to another century. Her reaction might appear unduly extreme until we examine in detail what we know of her life as a whole.

Apparently when Alphonse first met her she had just been abandoned by a 'useless braggart' who had led her a 'vile life'. This was in September 1939. As if to emphasise his insensitivity, Alphonse tells this story to her and she interrupts him with 'But that is our story.' When they had got to know each other, he helped

Bernard on the cliff-top →

Hélène with the tailor and his wife

her and gradually they fell in love. Since it was, in a sense, thera-
peutic and signalled a new kind of life for Hélène, his love for her
was more important to her than it would normally have been.
When their love affair broke up, after what seemed to her (or she
had managed to persuade herself was) an accident, she had to
continue to believe he loved her despite circumstantial evidence
to the contrary, because without such a belief her life would revert
to its former misery.

The actual circumstances of their break are vague. Alphonse
insists that he wrote to her to meet him at the Globe d'Or, just
after the war, to be his wife. He kept the appointment but she did
not. Hélène says she did not get the letter. Later in the film,
Ernest reveals that it was he who wrote to her to meet him at the
Globe d'Or. Ernest wanted to marry her, but Alphonse did not
post his letter. Just as the statue in *Marienbad* has two interpretations, both Alphonse's and Ernest's stories fit the facts; but in

view of the rest of Alphonse's behaviour, we, the audience, and Hélène are bound to believe Ernest.

In the years of separation she has clung to the myth of his fidelity to sustain her, and has lived very largely in the past. Her interests (antiques) have been past-directed, but even so she has not been entirely successful in keeping away a feeling of insecurity. Her early suffering has reasserted itself. Perhaps she has not been quite so committed to self-deception that she has been able wholly to believe in Alphonse's love. As a result she has become a compulsive gambler. (Cayrol has done his psychological reading on this point.)

When Alphonse arrives, she is more interested in their past than in the possibility of a future for them together. She needs to believe in the continuity of his love, but she does not really need his presence. She wrote to him to confirm her fantasy, not for him to share her old age. When this prop is removed by Ernest, she disintegrates. The love of de Smoke cannot replace it, for although he is loyal, he was not her first lover and he did not reclaim her to life. Also de Smoke is a figure of the present. His business is to demolish the old Boulogne to make room for the new. In Hélène's life, therefore, he represents present reality which threatens her past-directedness. Only her love for Bernard might express the need she has for reassurance; but he has murdered a man and has to leave town.

Hélène's mistake is to rely exclusively upon one experience in her life to build her security on. But no single experience is profound enough to bear such a structure, so she has to build around it a fantasy of perfection which will give it strength and depth. Such a fantasy, however, is self-defeating because it rivets the emotional orientation of the woman on one time period among the many in her life. Her life before and after this affair have been sacrificed to it, mere adjuncts whose only purpose is to testify to its authenticity. Like the girl from Nevers, though far less intensely, her emotional development has been arrested, frozen in one time; and like X in *Marienbad* she maintains a fantasy around a love affair that was not quite as perfect as she would like to believe.

Delphine Seyrig with Jean-Pierre Kérien and (*opposite*) Claude Sainval (de Smoke)

She has no durational sense and is, in fact, not free. Not only is her gambling compulsive, she does not live as she would in conformity with a continuous view of her past and present, but as her mythical past demands: as a widow thinking continually of the past. As Bergson says: 'We are free when our acts spring from our *whole* personality, when they express it, when they have that indefinable resemblance to it which one sometimes finds between the artist and his work.' (*Time and Free Will*, p. 172.) Hélène's acts have nothing to do with her whole life (personality): they revolve around one relationship and so she is dominated and restricted by that one relationship. Ernest frees her from this domination and she is forced to face her freedom at last, but whether she will realise it is something that cannot be deduced from the film. All we know is that the revelation has rather shattered her, but that is only to be expected (compare Ibsen's *The Wild Duck*).

The other triangle centres on Bernard, Hélène's adopted son, who complied with the torture and murder of Muriel, an Algerian girl. His sense of guilt about this dominates his present life and prevents him from coming close to people around him, in a way that recalls the girl from Nevers. Like her, but more so, he is isolated within his own guilt. Whenever we see him we get the impression that he is absorbed in his own thoughts, and even when the world around does appeal to his consciousness, it is as an intruder and not as something basic to his experience. But, unlike the girl in *Hiroshima*, his feelings are not all directed towards himself. He does not suffer as she does, because he has found two ways of expressing his repressed emotions which alleviate his sense of guilt and lessen his pain.

He has invented an imaginary girl friend whom he calls Muriel, to replace the original. To some extent he can believe that the Algerian girl is not really dead, but more important than this, he can identify with this mythical Muriel. Significantly she is always ill, and by caring for her he takes upon himself her suffering and makes recompense for it. This new Muriel acts as a symbol and also an expression of his guilt. In another sense, she is the foundation of a private world which belongs to him and no one else. Even Hélène is excluded. She knows the name Muriel, but as Bernard says, 'Calling people by their first names isn't to know them.' And, of course, this Muriel is an ideal excuse to get away on his own. He also expresses his guilt through his vision of himself as a symbol of justice. His sense of guilt has hardened into a desire for revenge against Robert, the final side of the triangle and the unwitting catalyst who actually killed Muriel. By collecting evidence and killing his former friend, Bernard expiates his guilt (or seeks to), and makes his final break with the past.

Unlike the girl from Nevers, Bernard does not try to forget the past: he faces it and seeks to express and atone for his guilt, but he deceives himself as much as she does. For, in the end, he does not atone, since he kills Robert for the wrong reasons. Indeed when it comes to the point he does not want to kill Robert. He shouts to him to go back and does not kill him until the last

Bernard in his secret room with Marie-Do (Martine Vatel)

moment. We feel that he shoots Robert more from panic than intention.* Perhaps he even uses the business of collecting evidence to *avoid* the act of murder. As long as he is still collecting, as long as his evidence is incomplete and unknown to anyone else, he can postpone acting upon it. But when the tape is accidentally played at Hélène's party, the evidence is disclosed and he feels publicly committed to action. This accounts for his exaggerated reaction to what, after all, was an accident—and not a very revealing one at that.

Bernard can only face the past by trying to lessen his guilt through the fantasy of the new Muriel and by placing the whole blame on Robert. This is dishonest. He should accept his own guilt and accept that *he* cannot expiate it, whatever he does. We

---

* Robert's attempts to pressure him into the O.A.S. movement are part of the reason why Bernard eventually acts.

cannot seek out redemption. All we can do is accept our guilt as a fact, place it in the whole context of our lives and realise that it is as much a sin to exaggerate it as to underrate it. In the future we must try to avoid similar acts of cowardice and simply try to do better. If we succeed, however, we should not look to heaven in anticipation of the hand of Divine Grace reaching down to forgive us. It might or might not be right for him to kill Robert (though of course, we want to ask, who is he to judge, especially when he is guilty of much the same crime), but that is not the point; what is at issue is that he should not use Robert to evade his own guilt. Hélène unwittingly makes the crucial point against Bernard when she tells him, 'You don't blame yourself for anything.'

While the concerns of Hélène with her antique shop and her former lover are directed towards the past, the purposes of Bernard with his desire for revenge and atonement, and of Robert with his O.A.S. interests, are directed towards the future. Hélène's feeling for the future is shallow compared with her roots in the past; and Bernard is now (what he was *immediately* after the death of Muriel is probably another matter) only interested in the past as a means of collecting evidence against Robert.* There are some people who are so full of revenge, they forget the injustice that gave rise to it.

Bernard's problems follow from his tendency to fragment the past, a fault which we have discovered in the protagonists of all Resnais' feature films. He has failed to provide the Muriel episode with a context, but instead of allowing it to torture him he has channelled it into a desire for action. It does, of course, dominate him, but his existence is not frozen at that one time, as those of

---

* 'We believe that we have analysed our feeling, while we have really replaced it by a juxtaposition of lifeless states which can be translated into words.' (*Time and Free Will*, p. 133.) This aptly sums up Bernard's mania for collecting evidence. His concern to 'translate' a vital past experience into the 'lifeless' jottings in notebooks, tape-recorded sounds and newspaper clippings with which he surrounds himself, is to allow intellect to dominate intuition. He uses this business to evade genuine feeling.

Hélène, X, and the girl from Nevers are. He has developed, moved ahead, but in a way that pays scant respect to his own responsibilities and to the significance of the episode in his own development. Rather, he has come to associate the agony of Muriel with the guilt of Robert and with the avenger in himself. If he had achieved a sense of duration, then his life afterwards would have taken a different course from the one we see in the film. But his life has gone off tangentially and has not proceeded directly from the episode. He has responded to the situation intellectually, trying to discover a means by which he could make recompense for it, instead of instinctively allowing its significance to impregnate his life as a whole.

Resnais overlaps and relates these two triangles continually. The parallels between the structure and the two sets of relationships are fairly obvious. Alphonse and Ernest share a similar past with Hélène as its object, as do Bernard and Robert with Muriel as its object. And as Hélène becomes the shared object of the two older men in the present, so Marie-Do becomes the mistress of both Robert and Bernard in the present or the near past. Hélène's fantasies about Alphonse are destroyed by Ernest the catalyst, as Bernard's fantasies about Muriel are destroyed by Robert the catalyst.

To a lesser extent, Hélène has been abused as was Muriel; and Bernard's war experiences have something in common with those of Alphonse. They are both dishonest and far from reality in their memories of the war. Bernard, describing the torture of Muriel, shows a film of soldiers celebrating Christmas or some such festival. The film is quite pleasant and is about as close as Bernard can now get to personal involvement in the war. Alphonse is even more cynical. All he can provide is a handful of conventional colour photographs and a lot of dishonesty about his role in the Algerian conflict. Both, in their own ways, evade responsibility for the war and their own behaviour in it. Alphonse even goes so far as to extol war and to say that it was a good life for him. Perhaps it was: he is just the kind of man to profit by war. No mere Mother Courage he! Moreover, there is a suggestion that Alphonse might

Images of Boulogne

have tortured someone. If there is some resemblance between Bernard and Alphonse, there is even more between Alphonse and Robert, who for sheer brutal insensitivity is quite his equal. Later in the film, Bernard meets his *bête noire*, Robert, at the same time and place that Alphonse meets with his, Ernest.

As well as drawing parallels in structure and content between the two triangles, Resnais uses the whole range of techniques to relate them. For example, simultaneous narrative is achieved by overlapping dialogue and intercutting. Significant moments are indicated on the soundtrack by the clavichord. And by having each character make tours of, and journeys through, the town, either alone or in pairs, Resnais establishes their interests and contrasts and compares their situations. Also, by using old and new Boulogne in relation to individual characters, he defines their roles in either triangle.

These parallels serve to reinforce the notion that successive generations duplicate each other's responses. Nothing really changes, except details: the form remains the same. The basic emotional problems, provided by the need to remember or to forget painful experiences (and the difficulty of doing either) occur for every generation; and our 'solutions' to these problems are notably unoriginal. What is relevant for the soldier in Algeria today was relevant for the soldier in Indo-China yesterday. There is, in fact, a strong cyclical theme in *Muriel* which is summed up by Ernest's song 'Déjà'. This song, which is an expression of something close to Bergson's notion of perpetual flux, relates the passage of time which is so imperceptible and yet so fast that we are old before we know it. As Ernest sings, we see shots of the new Boulogne rising from the scarred city of the days when Hélène and Alphonse were young. As Beckett puts it, 'we give birth astride the grave'; but this epigram has a corollary that makes dying a prerequisite of being born. The circle always completes itself.

So, as a new Boulogne is built to replace the old ruined city that was once itself new and unscarred, new generations of Bernards and Muriels succeed the old disfigured generation of

Hélène and Alphonse who were once young and unmarked. And just as Bernard and Muriel have been tainted by life, so the new skyscrapers will become ruins in new wars. We are even given hints of this new force which will take the place of the Nazis who made the cities and the lives of earlier generations ugly. This new fascism is the O.A.S., as represented by Robert and his band of young men who might or might not be survivors from the Algerian war. Thus history repeats itself. The young make the same or similar mistakes as the old. And new buildings and cities share the fate of those they replace. Wars succeed wars; torture, torture; fascist armies, fascist armies. The new is new so that it may become old, and beauty is beautiful so that it may become ugly. Time the great destroyer reduces all to nothing. One of the conclusions of *Muriel* seems to be, 'There is no such thing as progress: there is only recurrence.' But why *must* this be so?

For the answer we must return to *Hiroshima Mon Amour*, to the inescapable fact which separated the man and the girl: the essential privacy of human experience. There is no progress because the young do not learn from the old, any more than the old learned from the older. Even when two sets of relationships are as similar structurally as those in *Muriel*, there is no contact. The apexes of the two triangles, Hélène and Bernard, learn nothing from each other. They have love and blood ties on their side as well as similar problems. Each lives a myth present based on a failure to face up to a past experience; both are 'visited', Hélène actually, Bernard through memory, by crucial figures from the past (Alphonse and Muriel); both find their fantasies destroyed by a catalyst figure who witnessed their past experience. But they remain isolated within their own pasts, unable to speak to each other. Resnais seems to say that the reason for this is not because they do not try: it is logically necessary in human beings. It follows from the nature of memory. Only something so necessary could account, for example, for Bernard's failure to learn, when he is involved in the problem of his own past not in isolation, but within the general context of Hélène's quest for her past. The past—in the shape of Alphonse and particularly Alphonse during the war—impinges on his

The lunch-party sequence, and intercut shots of Boulogne buildings as Ernest (Jean Champion) sings 'Déjà' →

consciousness and contributes to the sense of contemporaneity of tense that pervades his life and the film itself. Yet despite this he learns nothing.

Unlike its predecessors, *Muriel* does not merely revolve around several highly personalised pasts, but expresses *la durée* more generally by showing that the present in which any character operates is not simply 'his present', but something created, even in its durational quality, by other people's presents and pasts. This is another case of the trend towards objectivity in Resnais' latest film.

The central theme of Time, as the great destroyer, the great reducer and the great repeater, justifies Resnais' technique of exterior narrative. We are shown these half-dozen characters in midstream (of Time!), floating along the same currents; at different stretches of the river perhaps, but ultimately making for the same destination.* The only way to indicate their relative positions and their overall similarities is from above, not from inside any or all of them. As in all his films, Resnais' technique is superbly appropriate to his theme.

---

* Despite their concern with psychological time, both Bergson and Resnais do seem to accept uncritically the stream metaphor of time; and it is this metaphor which makes the idea of time as the great destroyer plausible. It is essentially a spatial metaphor, which leads us to hypostatise events and to postulate a series of time dimensions. By exploiting this kind of misleading image, Bergson is able to condemn certain intellectual processes and Resnais is able to find credible dilemmas to build films around.

4: La Guerre est Finie

La Guerre est Finie represents a development of Resnais' thought. In the three earlier feature films, his characters were essentially negative. We were shown men and women isolated in their pasts, without durational sense and with their lives in ruins, because they were unable to face present reality. Only Bernard tried to act dynamically in the present, and his efforts were so entirely misguided that his plans to atone were a hopeless mixture of cowardice, self-deception and dishonesty.

In *La Guerre est Finie*, the problem of what it is to act in accordance with one's past and with due past-directedness for one's future (durationally for Bergson; authentically for the Existentialists) becomes central. This question is an inevitable development of Resnais' previous theoretical concerns; and to Jorge Semprun, the expatriate Spanish socialist who wrote the screenplay, it emphasises the very practical demand that revolutionaries must, sooner or later, cash out their dreams in blood. It is formally appropriate that such a theme is developed in the setting of Spanish politics, because no other situation seems to combine such vivid memories of a political watershed with such persistent fantasies about the nature of present day society. By drawing upon these features of the last thirty years of Spanish history, Resnais is able to generalise about the illusions of a whole generation, and to contrast these illusions with the confident, but no less mistaken, beliefs of today's committed youth. And through

his central character, Resnais begins to show how human beings might assimilate their experience and escape the Bergsonian dilemma of the tension between the tenses. With Bernard we saw someone try and fail; with Diego the struggle is successful. While those around him fall into the political and ideological stereotypes which most of us use as substitutes for coming to terms with our personal experience, Diego confronts the inconsistencies of his life. He refuses, unlike many political extremists, to use the security of dogma to compensate for the difficulties of his private life. So, in that it deals with the psychological malaise of a whole generation, *La Guerre est Finie* has a breadth that was absent from Resnais' first two feature films and was only glimpsed at in *Muriel*.

Diego lives in a maze of illusions out of which he is trying to thread his way to some kind of reality. There is even something vague about his identity. His party name is Carlos; to Nadine he is Domingo; and his real name is Diego. Only Marianne calls him Diego: perhaps only she knows his real name, and even she only discovered it after being fed with a series of pseudonyms. Furthermore, he has several passports and spends long periods living under other people's identities. He is absent from his friends so much that Agnès, an acquaintance of Marianne, had 'begun to wonder if he really existed'. These kind of doubts about personal identity, and the specific forms that Diego's political difficulties assume, are more fruitfully described in Existentialist than in Bergsonian terms. Bergson does not provide an adequate account of what a notion of duration is; and in a sense this is quite proper, since the behavioural ideal varies with individual lives. Sartre, however, is crucially interested in what it is to be free and to act authentically. While Bergson gives us a philosophy of mental forms, Sartre articulates a philosophy of action.* And a philosophy of action is just what Diego is searching for.

---

* Bergson puts considerable emphasis on the ideal of action, but his view seems to be that action for its own sake is worthwhile. He does not tie the concept to a social, moral and psychological theory as Sartre does, but justifies it by reference to the somewhat vague notion of creative evolution.

Nadine: Geneviève Bujold

Spaniards in exile

I. As in the films of Jean-Luc Godard, the myth-reality theme is structured on several levels in *La Guerre est Finie*. Central is Diego's political life, which is riveted on his youthful experience in the Spanish Civil War. He has spent his life working for a revolutionary group which still thinks in terms of 1936 and appears not to have realised that thirty years have passed since there was last any hope for the Spanish people. By their behaviour the members of the group confirm the truth of Diego's remark that 'In the suburbs of Paris you can make the reality of Spain conform to your dreams.' But their Spain no longer exists: old men, they live in their youth, out of contact with the realities of the present day. As Diego says, they cannot put themselves in the place of Bilbao workers, so how can they presume to predict their behaviour? But like the girl from Nevers and Hélène, they have developed protective fantasies for themselves—in their case to cushion the hard facts about Franco's Spain. Year after year they persuade themselves, despite regular disappointments, that a general strike is imminent; and when there are a series of arrests in Madrid, they interpret the well-informed police swoops as being panic measures to prevent the inevitable success of their policy. Their attempts here to rationalise Diego's fears out of existence demonstrate, particularly forcefully, the extent of their delusions, because all the evidence is in Diego's favour. For instance, the arrests have been reported in the newspapers. It is unlikely that the Spanish authorities would have allowed this unless the reports were true, and they would hardly have given such fair warning to the rest of the group's agents unless they were confident that they could break up the whole network. Moreover, the arrests were not due to the usual kind of random police swoop. The authorities had attacked the network at several key points, which suggests they knew precisely what they were doing. Yet Diego's superiors wilfully maintain that the arrests prove the police fear the strike. They sustain themselves with bigoted newspapers and self-important but impotent committee meetings which enable them to live out existences that are nothing more than euphemisms for what life is really all about. Typical of Diego's superiors is Roberto, who 'hates reality for not conforming to his dreams,' and 'almost hates you for telling him the truth,' and 'hates bad news not because of the years of lost work or the comrades who have died, but because it brings him face to face with reality.'

Gradually Diego has managed to extricate himself from these illusions, and the governmental purge of the group's organisation in Madrid finally forces him to realise that 'Spain is no longer the dream of 1936 but the reality of 1965.' He refuses any longer to pay for the illusions of his leaders with the lives of his comrades and, on his own initiative, returns from Spain to save Juan's life. But instead of trying to keep Juan at Perpignan, Roberto says that Diego's report is exaggerated; a subjective judgement. This assessment is reaffirmed by the rest of the Paris group and Diego is relieved from returning to Madrid and advised to rest, to think things over.

The political uncertainty of Diego's activities as a professional

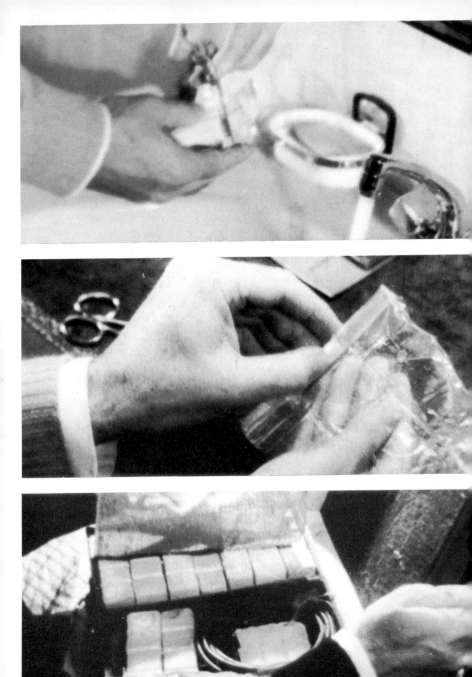

revolutionary is paralleled by the almost fictional nature of the social life he is forced to lead. He is burdened with false names, forged papers, temporary contacts, addresses which are used once or twice then changed, messages hidden in tubes of toothpaste. Even when he is with Marianne, who represents reality, this fantasy element occasionally intervenes. To explain to their friends his six months' absence in Spain, Marianne makes up the story that he has been in Brussels with the UN, while he tells them he has been in Rome with UNESCO. This deception, however, is immediately contrasted with Diego's talk about their walks among the fountains of the Piazza Navona, which revives for her the reality of their love.

Resnais' analysis of the self-deception of these exiled Spaniards has critical implications for the whole of left-wing politics. Just as Diego and his friends have been indulging their fantasies in the face of political realities, might not all Marxist-Anarchist revolutionaries be deluding themselves when they talk about revolution and socialism? In view of twentieth century history, this is a serious question for the Left; but there is a facile theoretical distinction which might enable young Leftists to escape its force. Diego and his companions, the argument would go, are special cases precisely because they are middle-aged and involved. They are not in a position to make a valid Marxist analysis of the Spanish situation, because of the cathartic experiences of their youth and because, as Spaniards, they are emotional when they should be objective.

Semprun defends himself against such criticism by showing that similar kinds of myths are held by a young French group of revolutionaries who have involved themselves in the Spanish Republican cause and who should have every reason, according to the Marxist case, for being rational about it.* Yet the only

---

* They even use the same jargon: 'objective—subjective analysis,' 'Lenin a dit,' etc. Lenin as a source which can be used to prove anything is neatly shown when Diego quotes him against the general strike policy, and his superior quotes Lenin to prove that Diego's opposition to the strike theory is based on a subjective judgement.

93

difference between them and the older revolutionaries is that, being younger, their fantasies tend to be more violent. They trot out the usual Leninist jargon as a substitute for thinking for themselves, and when Diego tells them that 'Lenin is not a praying wheel,' he is accused of having 'bourgeois pretensions'. And the practical policy which they have derived from 'an objective Marxist analysis' turns out to be an attempt to disrupt Spain's vital tourist trade by throwing a few plastic bombs around. Where? How many? As Diego comments, they might just as well try to 'switch off the sun.'

Diego's position, however, is not as simple as this. At the meeting the students score several debating points against him; not because their fantasy triumphs over his reality, but because he is by no means as free from the appeal of his own group as the above analysis has suggested. Although he is free from the illusions of his comrades, he still needs the group—its comradeship, its contacts with Spain and its involvement with left-wing politics. As he says, 'I didn't become a revolutionary to live my life in a French suburb.' So when the students attack his group, Diego defends the integrity of his comrades, not because he believes they are right, or even any less wrong than these young Leninists, but because they are his comrades and his countrymen. It is galling to have to listen to a group of over-confident young Frenchmen criticising middle-aged, crucially experienced Spaniards about how they are conducting their own revolution; however valid these criticisms may be. The debate is between the old and the new illusions, neither of which Diego now shares. And the criticisms of the young men, although he tries to answer them, only confirm his own disillusionment. For example, he defends the strike policy, in which he palpably disbelieves, by saying that six years is a short period to decide that a policy is valueless. But his response is one of irritation rather than conviction.

The make-believe quality of the young men's political ideas is paralleled, as are those of the older group, by the surreptitious lives they lead. To carry out their plans they have to live double lives: on the one hand as normal students, on the other all the paraphernalia of secret rendezvous, committee meetings to discuss strategy, carrying plastic bombs in suitcases, checking to make sure they are not being followed, etc. And what is more they involve Diego in this when he is in France. The point that Resnais and Semprun are making by the repeatedly emphasised parallel is that having revolutionary ideas involves a whole way of life; and to the extent that these ideas are false, so the way of life is phoney.

II. The conflicts and confusions of myth and reality in Diego's political life are reproduced in his sexual life. His brief affair with the young girl, Nadine, arises directly from his role as a professional revolutionary. He has used her father's passport (his identity!) for his recent trip to Spain, and when he is close to being discovered she proves that she can play the spy game as well as anyone, and over the telephone readily accepts the role of his daughter. She belongs to the unreal side of his life. In the course of making his contacts, dodging possible police tails and playing the spy game generally, he begins to wonder what she could be like. Resnais accomplishes this piece of interior monologue by flashing on to the screen images of different girls doing the kinds of things a student would do. The fact that he knows the girl— her biographical details, that is—before he even meets her suggests that she is less a person for him than an idea. Finally he goes to her home, ostensibly to see her father. The circumstances of this meeting thrust him into an immature sexual relationship and further bizarre political manoeuvres.

He makes love to her almost by chance, and in the treatment of the love scenes Resnais makes Nadine exhibit all the coyly affected shyness that we associate more with the sexual fantasies of Roger Vadim than with a genuine relationship between a man and a woman. Like Bardot she almost pouts over the top of the bedclothes. And in his extensive references to Godard's *Une Femme Mariée*, Resnais' stylised shots of limbs pale against the bedclothes take on some of the meaning Godard originally gave them; of a kind of ironic aestheticism rather than passion; of style rather than feeling. There is also a consciously teasing (satirical) quality about

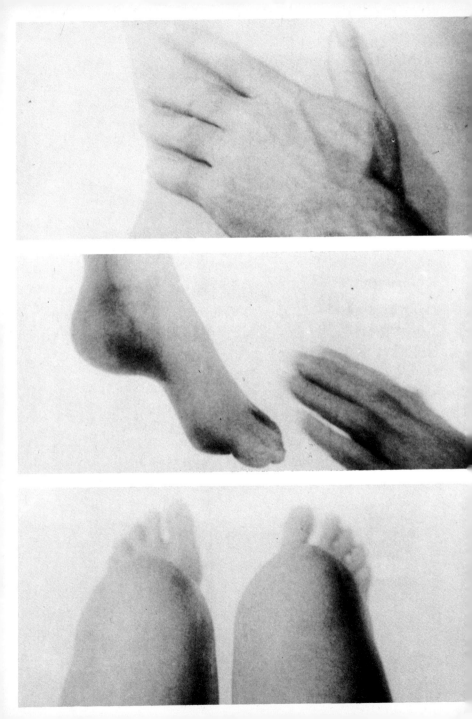

the shot of her knees opening which again reminds one more of Vadim's treatment of sex than Resnais'.

The immediate contrasting of all this is with Diego's love scenes with Marianne, but one also cannot help thinking how they differ from those of *Hiroshima*. And again Resnais uses overexposure throughout the scenes with Nadine, a technique which, as in *Marienbad*, represents unreality. In *Marienbad* it is unreality of an almost nightmarish intensity; here it is the unreality of a certain stereotyped notion of bliss. The girl appears to float, her body is incredibly white. This romanticises the moment of sexual release in a highly clichéd manner. The unreality of the mystical nature of Nadine's orgasm compares unfavourably with the strongly sensual pleasure that is apparent on Marianne's face. There are shades of Bergman here, but not, I think, of cynicism.

Continuing his habit of hiding his real identity, Diego is unable to tell her his correct name* and contents her with the name Domingo. This immediately acquires another layer of fantasy when she remarks that it means Sunday, which becomes his code name to her in the series of intrigues in which they become involved together. With Nadine everything turns to intrigue. Indeed, the 007 side of his life is one of the strongest attractions he has for her. Admiringly she affirms 'You're a professional—*formidable*!' So it is hardly surprising that in view of her immature admiration for him, his sexual contact with her seems to be unsatisfying. When he leaves Nadine after making love to her, instead of appearing to be content, he immediately thinks about Marianne in an image which is intentionally sexual.

By contrast with Nadine, Marianne represents reality. His affair with her has nothing to do with his political life; indeed she is excluded from it, both by himself and by the dislike his comrades show for her. She involves him in no intrigues but presents him with a normal life with normal friends (photographer) and interests (cinema, literature, etc.). If any intrigue does encroach upon

---

* As he says later, 'I am startled when I hear my own name': a remark which is almost psychotic in its psychological implications.

Images of unreality: the love scene with Nadine

their life, it is Diego who involves her in it and not vice versa. She has never even been to Spain. She is outside the political game. With her he can be reasonably himself. She knows his real name, and he can talk to her about his feeling for Spain and his discontent with his group's politics.

Throughout the earlier part of the film, all his sexual images are of Marianne, and when they meet their sexual need for each other dominates. Their love scenes are filmed realistically, erotically and movingly. Marianne's clothes don't ideally disappear when required as do Nadine's, but have to be removed with a natural incongruity which leaves her headscarf on until almost the last moment. The positioning of their bodies is not beautiful but natural, with the touches of absurdity that love-making must provide, seen objectively. The performance is not too neat to be unreal. Resnais concentrates on physical details and particularly on the passion of their encounter. We have the impression that they have actually made love; an impression which is absent from the scenes with Nadine. However, there is more than sensuality in the love sequence between Diego and Marianne. While the scenes with Nadine have a phoney mystical quality about them, there is something almost reverential in the way that he makes love to Marianne. The way he takes hold of her crossed feet suggests certain religious imagery, and this is affirmed through the musical score. We hear the leitmotif (Diego's Spanish music) which occurs only when he is in contact with what he loves: we hear it at the opening of the film when he is near the Spanish border, and at Ramon's funeral. This music which sounds like a Kyrie captures something of the spirituality of his feelings. In contrast, the scenes with Nadine are backed by a high-pitched violin which mocks what we see on the screen. Spain and Marianne, or rather his love of both, are again clearly connected by the visual images of the fiery shadows that flicker across the ceiling as he lies on the bed thinking of Spain and later at the climax of his love-making with Marianne.

Afterwards they talk as people do. She wants to bear his child, the continuing reality of his presence; she does not admire him as

Images of reality: Marianne (Ingrid Thulin) and Diego (Yves Montand)

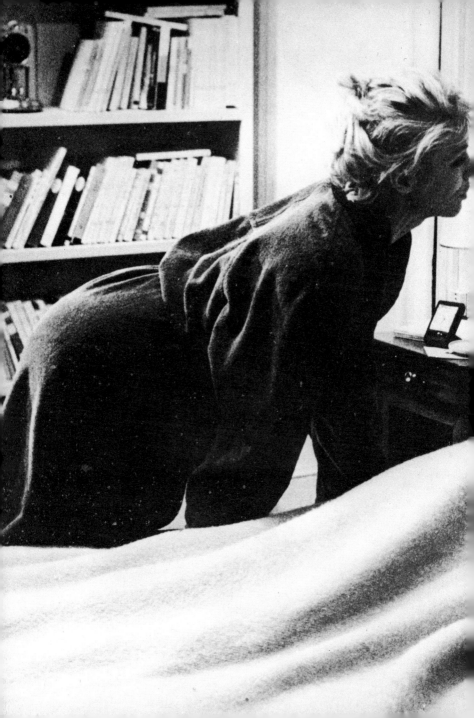

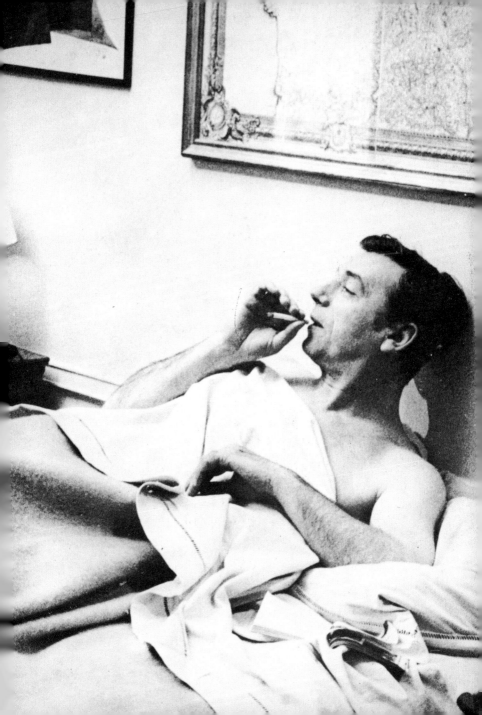

a revolutionary, a vocation which to her is as unreal as it is irritating. She admits being attracted to others, but affirms her special feeling for him. She is real, a woman, and after he has made love to her he is satisfied, physically and emotionally. Quite typically afterwards he demands food, his next physical priority. Marianne is Resnais' first well-adjusted woman, as Diego is his first well-adjusted man. She is concerned with people, not with ideas, just as Diego, the political animal, thinks more about saving the lives of his comrades than about engineering strikes. All his memory/imagination flashes are either of her or of his comrade Juan, whose life is in danger. Never once do we see him thinking about his political hopes.

III. We must not think that only revolutionaries (old or new) live in a bogus world, or more precisely a bogus Spain. Year after year 14,000,000 holidaymakers go to Spain for the sun, the cheap food and drink, the architecture and the traditions; and while they enjoy all these things, they close their minds to the conditions of the peasantry and the nature of the Spanish government. They enthuse about the legend of Lorca, but ignore his opinions and the circumstances of his death. The reality of Spain, a country ruled over by a dictator whose authority was imposed with the support of the fascist régimes of Germany and Italy, and is maintained by the suppression of free speech, by press censorship and by secret police, fades beside the colourful advertisements urging us to bask on the Costa del Sol. As Diego says, to most of us Spain is just a 'tourists' paradise all mixed up with the myth of the Civil War.' *We* suffer from a self-deception which is arguably far more immoral than that of Diego's friends, because while they deceive themselves that they can change an atrocious situation, we as tourists deceive ourselves so that we can enjoy the sun and the wine of Spain without the bothersome pangs of conscience. Their illusions arise from a drive to do good, ours from an urge to pure pleasure.

In this context, then, Diego is torn two ways over Spain and over his comrades. He has emerged mentally from the political myths, although behaviourally he is still involved in the political intrigues. But, on the other hand, he is a Spaniard who loves Spain and cannot feel completely at ease anywhere else. And certainly a Bergsonian would say that to cut himself off from Spain would be to deny his past, which would be as great an error as to be over-whelmed by it. Moreover, he is politically committed and he could not even bear to live in Spain as a law-abiding citizen, a possibility which he and Marianne consider. To do so would entail leaving his political group and losing the friends whose company has sustained him in the years of exile. No longer would 'the doors open' and 'the faces greet' him. And while even this comfort is unreliable (the Ramons die and the widows move), it is all he has left of Spain.

Marianne tells him quite correctly that he 'does not know where (he) is going.'* He can no longer fool himself as Roberto and company do, but if he deserts them he will give up every chance of changing their views. As he remarks satirically, 'Patience and irony are the principal virtues of the Bolshevik.' A good Marxist would remain in the Party, appearing to affirm its policies but secretly waiting until he could alter them. This is what Lenin, Marx or Trotsky would have done, but it is also what Stalin *did* do. Although he is annoyed by the way his superiors make use of him, one moment censuring him and the next ordering him to risk his life, Diego is willing to return to Spain to save Juan—although, at first, he accepts the assignment without having solved his problems *vis à vis* the Party.

Only when Ramon dies does Diego acquire the insight that enables him to tolerate the Party without either embracing its illusions or rejecting it as totally valueless. Ramon the man whose

---

* Until Ramon's funeral he is so confused about his personal and political future that he becomes careless. For instance he rebukes Nadine for driving without her lights on, then a little later he is stopped by the police for the same offence. In a man usually so methodical (e.g. the way he smooths his notepaper at the committee meeting; the care he takes in checking his expenses and destroying all the evidence of his recent trip to Spain), this is a serious indication of his anxiety.

Ramon (Jean Bouise) with his wife

parents were Spanish but who had never been to his homeland, Ramon the good-natured friend with his 'Breton', Ramon the good comrade who is a human being not a dogmatist: Ramon has died before he can go to Spain and contact Juan, and Diego must take his place. Ramon represents for Diego what is worthwhile about the group and about the life of a revolutionary. He was self-effacing, prepared to perform run-of-the-mill jobs such as hiding pamphlets in cars, when he would rather have gone to Spain. When Diego told his news to Roberto, Ramon immediately offered to go to Barcelona—'it would be a change.' He accepted discipline but did not appear to share the illusions of his group. He brought some kind of normality (he is the only revolutionary we see in a family context) to the political scene; not by his ideas—because he does not appear to have any—but by his feelings. For Ramon, Spain and his Spanish friends were real, and beside this fact, the theory and the intrigue were not important. This is a truth Diego learns when he hears of his friend's death—which was not dramatic, at the hands of Franco's secret police, but the result of something as commonplace as a heart attack.

The spirit of Ramon enters Diego. He vows that he will see Spain again through the dead man's eyes, as if he were seeing it for the first time. 'You will be watching the vineyards with him.' The feeling which each comrade has for the others, beneath the wrangling, is what Diego needs. This is what Spain means to him and it is what the revolution is all about. Love for one's countrymen and one's homeland is what holds them together. It is concrete and real in marked contrast to the abstract ideals of the young Leninists. The solemnity of Ramon's funeral, backed on the soundtrack by Diego's Spanish theme, is placed against the callous remark of the student that 'cemeteries make for open spaces.' 'You should have told him to be silent,' Diego thinks to himself. Such youthful cynicism appals him, and the students' predilection for violence convinces him that his preference for his own group is right. When he walks out on the students he warns them that 'all those who play the terrorist game have had it.' Roberto and the rest may be deluded, but their activities are harmful only to themselves and their friends, whereas these students are dangerous. They are callous and fanatical without any of the saving graces of genuine feeling which are found in Ramon and Diego and which exist beneath the vagaries of the other Spanish revolutionaries. The impatience of the students even disqualifies them from being judged good Leninists (Bolsheviks). But his own leaders are patient and they represent the continuity of a tradition that is Spain for Diego. At the funeral he affirms that it is this Spain and not his own principles which is important. He can ignore the political absurdity for the truth of Spain. He will go to Madrid, die if necessary, to maintain contact with this reality, to sustain the vitality of this love.

If politically the Leninist students seem to him brutal and emotionally insensitive, similar failings are also apparent in Nadine. She is naïve and immature and so he leaves her. When she asks him when he will return, he does not answer—partly because he rejects her and partly because he believes he may not return. Just before he leaves, one of the group tells him that things are not as bad as they believed in Madrid. But the danger of the

Ramon's funeral, the drab procession in Paris merging into the seaside cemetery in Spain

mission is no longer of central importance. What is vital is the trip itself and the spirit in which he embarks on it. Ironically his cover name turns out to be Chauvin: ironical but not inappropriate. He departs calmly, even cheerfully, because he has made his decision. Spain comes first and the group is his means of contact with Spain. Theory must be rejected when it conflicts with duty: violence must always be rejected and love always affirmed. And of all the people who care about Spain, his own comrades, despite their fantasies, are the least callous, the least violent, the most involved and the most feeling. So he must continue to work with them for Spain and trust that their humanity will triumph over their illusions and prevent them from unnecessarily sacrificing each other for the sake of useless policies.

Resnais might have chosen to close the film at this point, but although to do so would be naturalistically justifiable, it would have meant that, formally, *La Guerre est Finie* would be incomplete. By returning to Spain Diego is reaffirming feeling against theory and reality against illusion, but to have left him apart from Marianne would have been to cut him off from the supreme source of love and reality in the film. Thus Resnais is true to his theme when he ends with Marianne following Diego to Spain; but the way this is managed seems to be implausible.

In the final ten minutes of the film everyone becomes more realistic. Nadine helps to provide information which makes the leaders of Diego's group realise that there is danger for him in Spain. This action is opposed to the role she played earlier when she helped to support the myth of his identity as her father. Nothing is said about Madrid: as far as we ever know, Diego's fears may have been needless though justified at the time. The danger to Diego springs from the very border incident in which Nadine played so significant a part. Diego was mistaken when he believed that the French frontier police questioned him by chance; that they habitually stopped black Citroëns. Apparently they had been warned about him by the Spanish police, who plan to allow him into Spain on his latest trip but will pick him up when he

The funeral sequence: Yves Montand, Yvette Etiévant

tries to leave. Presumably they will wait so that they can get Juan as well.

So Marianne is to go to Spain to tell him and Juan to return to France by a different route. And with Marianne involved we have reality entering the political arena. She goes for the very human purpose of saving lives, not to indulge in political intrigue. Perhaps also Resnais implies that she represents France symbolically*

---

* Symbolically at most, because although she is resident in Paris, Marianne is not French.

Leninist students' meeting

accepting responsibility for her neighbour's situation. With Marianne beside him ('*his* Breton'!), Diego is not likely to become deluded. Moreover, the fact that the group at last trusts Marianne suggests an improvement, the breaking down of one mystique: that only Spaniards have a part to play in Spanish politics. They have come one step closer to 1965.

This about turn is perhaps the only unconvincing feature of the whole film. It is hard to believe that such men would be changed, suddenly, by a single truth. It is quite easy to accept something as true, and even to act on it, without experiencing its force. And on a practical level, why of all people send Marianne? Is it plausible that Roberto and company would choose an inexperienced foreigner whom they had previously disliked and distrusted? It might be argued that they are short of agents, or that all their men are known or might be known to the Spanish police, so that it is vital, with the pressure on, to send someone who is neither

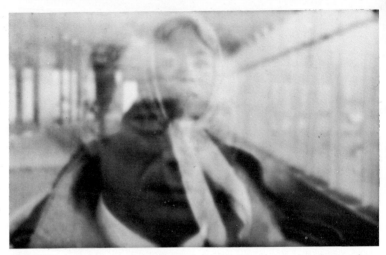

The final sequence: Marianne at the airport. Dissolve as her face replaces Diego's

Spanish nor experienced because such a person is less likely to be suspected. All this is possible, but to maintain it is to give the film the benefit of a very strong doubt. We are simply given no reason why they should trust her at the end of the film when they didn't earlier on. She has done nothing to merit their trust.

IV. The first thing one notices about all this is that the memory problem is no longer central. It is there as a condition of the film's development, but it is not discussed. Diego's superiors are typical of Resnais' earlier characters. Their lives are orientated by specific memories which fill their presents and will fill their futures, but Diego is struggling free of the constricting grasp of such memories. He is trying to create for himself a present Spain, a present life and a present identity which involve his former Spain, life and identity but are not stifled by them. He is reaching towards a sense of duration, which is apparent in Resnais' continual shots of his *imagination involontaire* which span and relate all aspects of his life. One cannot imagine Roberto, for instance, thinking about

anything but certain specific problems phrased in stereotyped images (voluntary, intellectualised, one might say teleological memory). Barcelona '36, Madrid '36, Guernica '37, Lorca, Picasso, La Pasionaria, etc. Roberto has intellectualised Spanish history and his own Spanishness. Bergson would condemn the young Leninists for much the same kind of intellectualism, only their memories are not even of real events, they are of chunks of text-books.

In contrast, Diego, in his Lorca speech, particularly rejects mythologising the past. In terms of Bergsonian jargon he has had certain pure perceptions* (e.g. a poster advertising holidays in sunny Madrid) which are then placed within the context of pure memories (e.g. the images of Franco's bombardment of Madrid, the rubble, the bodies, the panic) to become concrete perceptions (e.g. the data and the sense of his Lorca outburst). In this way the world becomes structured as the world of Diego's whole personal

---

* See page 15 for the full account of this procedure.

experience. And so, although he must reject the illusion of his comrades (the intellectualised notion of the world composed of voluntary memories), he must reaffirm his contacts with them and return to Spain, because to cut himself off from them would be to isolate his present from his past, fragment his experience and lose the sense of flow (duration) that he has begun to acquire.

Yet, unlike Mathieu in Sartre's *Les Chemins de la Liberté*, Diego does not risk his life for an idea. When Mathieu finally escapes from the straitjacket imposed by his own omnivorous rationality and realises that he is free, he can do nothing but die for the idea of his own freedom. Being free he does not know what to do with his liberty. He remains guilty of the bad faith of thinking about what he should do instead of living his own freedom. Diego, on the other hand, does not sacrifice himself for an idea. He has rejected the fragmented life of the intellect which possesses itself of a concept (the Party, the dogma, and so on) and subjects everything else to it. And so liberated, he rejects the urge to replace these ideas with another: Spain. His decision to return to Spain is in good faith, because his Spain is not an abstraction and because his decision is a reaffirmation of his Spanishness, of his values, of his loves, and of his past. He does not run to Spain to escape from himself or to opt out of his relationship with Marianne, but because what is real about his life and his love for her is co-extensive with the reality of Spain. He refuses to associate his consciousness solely with its objects, but maintains the mutuality of his 'being for itself' and 'being in itself' which is the essence of good faith.

Technically *La Guerre est Finie* is similar to Resnais' earlier films. It contains the same filmic devices as the three other features, but without the symbolic tightness of *Marienbad*, the narrative complexity of *Muriel* or the psychological depth of *Hiroshima*. With the exception of the first ten minutes, when the audience is lost within the topography of the film,* the action and

---

* The confusion here is completely justified formally. It evokes the strangeness and the disorder of the spy-revolutionary life more succinctly and vividly than all the contrived 'mystery' of more commercial features.

the problems of the characters are developed with a clarity that we have not come to expect of a Resnais film. (The other three films were never vague, but occasionally they were unclear.) The same visual devices constantly appear. Rapid cutting to correspond to involuntary memory and imagination, over-exposure, over-lapping dialogue to portray the connections between two scenes in the protagonist's mind, off-screen narration to represent interior monologue, and music which in *La Guerre est Finie* notably includes a choral leitmotif introduced on the guitar which trans-figures Diego's moments of profound feeling.

These are the characteristics of Resnais' cinematic style, which is by no means as complex or as difficult to learn as we have been led to understand. The technical subtleties of Resnais' films are almost always literary and especially structural. He is not an in-novator, but has created a personal style out of techniques which have long existed in the cinema. Moreover, his films have some kind of formal necessity, they contain an expression of social and political values in terms of profound psychological studies, they represent a genuine liaison between literature and the cinema and give evidence of a consistent philosophic attitude to the way we behave. These are his virtues and they are such that they would rate him considerable respect in the literary world. In the over-valued environment of the modern cinema, they make him the finest film-maker to have emerged since the war.

Diego and Nadine →

5: Resnais and his Sources

Sooner or later, anyone who grasps the virtual dialectical unity of Resnais' films begins to wonder how he manages it. The films are so personal that it seems impossible he did not write the scripts himself. But we know that he is no *auteur* in the strict sense, and that his scripts come from several writers whose theoretical and stylistic concerns are highly diverse. He appears to have a close working relationship with his writers even before he begins to shoot the actual films. Marguerite Duras and Alain Robbe-Grillet affirm this in their published scripts, and Resnais himself, in an interview with Pierre Wildenstein of *Téléciné*, admits that he suggested to Duras the idea of writing a film script about a love affair in Hiroshima with reference to a previous tragic affair with a German soldier in occupied France. Still, this does not entirely explain the detailed unity of his work, which would be surprising from a collaboration with a single writer, let alone with four.

The key to this enigma lies in the interest which each of his writers has consistently shown in the concepts of time, memory and the past, particularly in their destructive or restrictive contexts; an interest which has most likely been increased under Resnais' influence. And a central fact of French literature—that no one can deal with these concepts without betraying Bergson's influence.

With the exceptions of Nietzsche and Marx, the most seminal figure that modern philosophy has produced for literature is Bergson. Joyce, Virginia Woolf, Shaw, Dorothy Richardson,

Svevo, Stein, Faulkner and Pirandello are all to different extents in his debt, but his most powerful influence has been in his own country. Since the great period of his popularity in the first twenty years of this century, with such novelists and poets as Proust, Gide, Péguy, Jules Romains, Barrès and Claudel, limited Bergsonians have appeared regularly in French literature. This does not mean that Cayrol, Butor, Cocteau or even Sartre, for example, have necessarily read and accepted Bergson's philosophy, but rather that his thought has become part of the French way of thinking about certain topics. He was one of the few philosophers who have managed to seize on conceptual problems that are essential to the existential concerns of their epoch. As a result, he has popularised these problems to such an extent that few writers who care about the condition of modern man can fail to deal in part with them, and in a manner which is markedly Bergsonian.

As a key figure in the anti-rational movement at the turn of the century, to which he contributed a metaphysic while Freud provided a psychological superstructure, Bergson must be considered as one of the progenitors of the stream of consciousness novel, surrealism and Sartrean Existentialism. These varied influences were possible because the Zeitgeist which Bergson helped to form has many strands. Rejection of intellect in favour of life and experience, particularly mental life which is characterised by its continuity and its susceptibility to intuitive understanding, is neatly compatible with the belief that through dreams, drugs or automatic response we can arrive at some deeper awareness of ourselves. The external world represents a threat to man's personal identity. Intelligence is powerless to defend this; so we must turn inward to discover the vitality of our lives. And when we do so we shall find impulses, ideas and symbols which will at first confuse us but which, as we come to be more familiar with them, will form patterns and meanings which make up our true selves. And at the same time this 'plunge into ourselves', our memories and our pasts, will teach us that we are free and enable us to rediscover our capacity for action and the community between ourselves and others.

In literature this has given rise to several precepts which have

Delphine Seyrig and Robert Hossein in *La Musica*, the first film directed by Marguerite Duras (with Paul Seban)

revolutionised novelistic technique. Consolidating the nineteenth century developments which stem from Baudelaire, Bergson provided a framework within which writers were able to assimilate the data of psychoanalysis and capture with increasing subtlety 'a multitude of secondary impressions impinging on the present moment of experience.' (*Bergson and the Stream of Consciousness Novel*, by Shiv K. Kumar,★ p. 31.) So, clock time has been shattered and the mental time of interior monologue, streamed consciousness and associated ideas has taken its place. And together with the breakdown of ordinary time has gone the breakdown of language. Both are creations of constricting intellect. Ordinary language has been replaced by the language of the absurd, the language of the unconscious and dreams, and even by new languages, in order to escape the old 'static and lifeless' categories and create a 'ceaseless process of becoming'. Finally, since 'the primary intention of the new novelist is to immerse himself completely, with a stupendous effort of imagination, in the stream of his

---

★ Blackie and Son, London 1962

character's consciousness so that he ceases to have any point of view of his own' (Kumar), the principle of Authorial Omniscience has been rejected (compare Sartre and Robbe-Grillet).

As a result, the novel (and the cinema) cannot be the same again. Resnais' scriptwriters have been affected by these changes in terms both of technique and content, even when they are apparently reacting against them, as we shall see.

The novels of Marguerite Duras are characterised by the same static mood, the sense of impending tragedy, often reinforced (as in *The Little Horses of Tarquinia* and *The Afternoon of Mr Andesmas*) by the stifling heat of summer about to be broken by rain, which we find in *Hiroshima*. The wait for rain in *Little Horses* and the actual rain in the film are both used to capture the tension between the central characters. In most of her work, location tends to dominate. Her characters appear to be stimulated more by place and setting than they are by each other; and certainly in *Hiroshima* the relationship between the man and the girl could not have developed without the constant stimulation of Hiroshima and the memories of Nevers. Nor is the girl from Nevers unique in Duras' fiction. In *The Square* there is another girl who has deliberately placed herself in a state of suspended psychic animation, subduing the 'life force' and rejecting any experience that might distract her from the singleness of her purpose. She has sacrificed herself to the ideal of a husband, as the girl from Nevers has sacrificed herself to the ideal of her past lover.*

Although it would be absurd to claim a philosophical alignment of Duras and Bergson, it is true that she works within the tradition to which he has notably contributed. Her fictional work invariably shows time both creating and isolating individual personalities. Time is the destroyer of our identities since it stratifies life if we allow it to do so. So in *The Square* we are presented with the commercial traveller who remembers by the seasons, by the blossom on the trees, the fruit in the markets, and can grasp no kind of personal continuity in his life. And in *Day in the Trees*, the old woman can say 'It happened suddenly in the winter two years ago. One morning I looked at myself in the mirror and I did not recognise myself.' Duras associates boredom with the passage of time, which dulls her characters' awareness of the point of their lives and relationships. Yet her novels rarely end without approaching something close to optimism. This is accomplished by lifting the curtain of the familiar—which obscures other people with a confused mass of objects, words and habit responses—to reveal through half intuited impressions and memories the nature of human relationships. Very appropriate to Duras' novels is Bergson's remark: 'As the self thus refracted and thereby broken to pieces is much better adapted to the requirements of social life in general and language in particular, consciousness prefers it and gradually loses sight of the fundamental self.' (*Time and Free Will*, p. 128.)

Although her books are packed with dialogue, she seems to distrust articulation. She seems to believe that people realise their

---

* I am by no means sure that this is how Marguerite Duras would see *The Square*, but I suspect this is how it might appear to a Bergsonian.

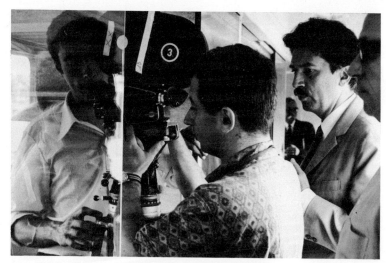

Alain Robbe-Grillet (*right*) directing *Trans-Europ Express*

closeness to each other through the sameness of their needs, which
are revealed by the responses they make to crucial situations in
their lives. It is not difficult to see how, when under Resnais'
prompting she came to deal with more Bergsonian subject matter,
the synthesis contained in *Hiroshima Mon Amour* was achieved.

We have already seen how Robbe-Grillet's ideas in *Marienbad* are
compatible with Bergson's position, but the argument was attenu-
ated for the sake of expositing the film. This is the time to dispel
certain mistaken notions about Robbe-Grillet's work and his
relation in general to the philosopher. These errors have been
propagated as much by Robbe-Grillet himself as by the critics.
According to both, Bergson is the archetype of the kind of thinker
with whom Robbe-Grillet is most out of sympathy. Certainly the
philosopher's views about the role of memory and intellect, indeed
his whole attempt to analyse consciousness from the inside, would
be condemned by the novelist, as would his theories of creative
evolution, *élan vital* and *la durée* as an emotional continuity. He

would reject, in other words, the metaphysic, the philosophy of mind; but so have many of the writers (e.g. Sartre and Ionesco) who have quite clearly been influenced by Bergson in other ways.

The source of most misconceptions about Robbe-Grillet's work has been his famous denunciation of interior monologue and his apparent rejection of character and the subjective novel. This seems to have been interpreted to mean that he refrains completely from analysing his characters' consciousnesses. He is concerned with what is seen, with the physical world and only that. What most critics have failed to realise is that he does not reject character, psychology and emotion any more than traditional novelists have done: the thesis of *chosisme* merely entails that these conceptions must be described by means other than introspection, direct description or stream of consciousness, which are all unreliable techniques because they cannot be checked and because they separate the reader from the novels. Character and so on must be created indirectly, through perception. *L'école du regard* does not refer to an ontological belief but to a theory of novelistic technique.

The point is summed up by Ben F. Stoltzfus in his book* on Robbe-Grillet as follows: 'Even though superficially this technique of the visual would seem to negate any concern with depth psychology . . . it does in fact project the subconscious on to these objects. This is done in two ways: first of all in terms of the selectivity of the protagonist (the tendency to perceive what is most meaningful to a particular state of mind), and secondly in terms of the objective correlatives which the author manipulates in order to reveal the state of mind of the protagonist' (p. 10). Examples of this last point are the descriptions in *Le Voyeur* of pieces of string, a rusty piton, figure eight shapes and surging waves, which with their genital and rhythmic associations reveal Mathias' pathological sexuality.† Thus Robbe-Grillet does delineate the inner psycho-

---

* *Alain Robbe-Grillet and the New French Novel*, South Illinois University Press, 1964.

† The theory behind this attempt to link perception and emotional states is perfectly respectable. For, of course, we do not just see whatever we encounter, we see what we are predisposed to see. We select.

Françoise Brion in Robbe-Grillet's *L'Immortelle*

logical world of his characters and their consciousness. There is a strong subjective element in his novels, since the perceptions are those of his characters; although this is fused to an element in which Robbe-Grillet's choice of objective correlatives indicates the protagonists' lack of freedom. Consider, for example, such objective correlatives as the match game, the geometrical gardens and the maze-like corridors in *Marienbad*.

Stoltzfus does not consider the relationship between Bergson and Robbe-Grillet, but it is clear from what has already been said that many of the objections against such an association have been removed. The denial of interior monologue and *analyse psycho-logique* no longer seems as important as at first sight. As for the positive points of similarity between the two Frenchmen, we can begin with Robbe-Grillet's doctrine of 'tragic complicity'. Like Bergson before him he diagnoses man's psychological sickness in terms of his tragic complicity with things. For him this takes the

Trans-Europ Express: Jean-Louis Trintignant, Marie-France Pisier

form of anthropomorphising physical objects so that we become their prisoners. Nature becomes our accomplice in the crimes we commit against each other and against ourselves. We try to find meanings in the external world and, like X in *Marienbad*, we become victims of confusion. We become alienated from ourselves. The only way we can become free is to keep a distance between ourselves and objects. It can be left to the reader how much Robbe-Grillet's opinions on this subject owe to a tradition of which Bergson, Husserl and Sartre are three important figures.

Together with most of the literary innovators of this century, Robbe-Grillet also shares Bergson's distinction between clock time and mental time. Mathias in *Le Voyeur* is significantly a watch salesman, but the narration of that story proceeds by a total dislocation of clock time intended to render 'this mental time which interests us, with its strange attributes, its gaps, its obsessions, its obscure regions, because this mental time relates our passions and our life' (*Realities*).*

---

* This sentence is repeated almost word for word in his introduction to the script of *L'Année Dernière à Marienbad*.

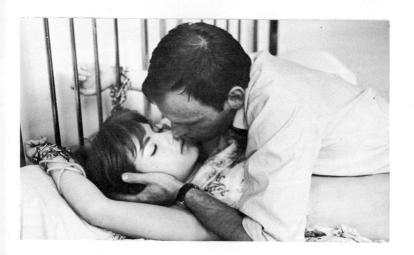

In *Les Gommes*, Wallas' watch has stopped at 7.30 p.m.: clock time has been suspended and psychological time is allowed to take its place. Robbe-Grillet, through the medium of perceptions, portrays the associations of his protagonists' minds as past memories or future daydreams and thereby reproduces their dislocated mental lives. In accomplishing this, he vividly portrays the malaise which Bergson has diagnosed.

The basic point of technique on which Robbe-Grillet is at odds with Bergsonism is that shared by Resnais himself: the reliance upon associationism in some form or other. In the novelist's case this takes the form of a recurrence of perceptual associations which are so organised as to reveal mental functioning; and so is entirely compatible with the more orthodox psychological associationism of Resnais himself. The natural bridge between Robbe-Grillet and Bergson, however, might be found in the theories of perception enunciated by the Gestalt psychologists. But, even without introducing holistic notions, the technique of associating perception and mental occurrence seems to have been anticipated in Bergson's concept of concrete perception. What Robbe-Grillet achieves by

Le Coup de Grâce, first film directed by Jean Cayrol →

portraying the selectivity of a character's perceptions ('certain images are made to stand out from an indifferent background of virtual perceptions as the explicit horizon of the self's experience of the world'; I. W. Alexander, *Bergson*, 1900), together with the use of objective correlatives, is similar to Bergson's formula: pure perceptions plus pure memory equals concrete perceptions.

Robbe-Grillet has tried to react against the tradition which was outlined at the beginning of this chapter, but he is not a theorist of sufficient stature to overthrow it completely. Consequently, by concentrating his criticism upon those features of the twentieth century novel which are markedly psychological, he has been compelled to fall back, through his failure to find anything genuinely new, upon the more purely philosophical aspects of the Bergsonian tradition.

The case of Jean Cayrol presents a rather different problem. Unlike Duras, Robbe-Grillet and Semprun, he introduced a fundamental idea into the script he wrote which it is difficult to believe Resnais agrees with. Of all the films, *Muriel* is the most pessimistic. It alone has a Weltanschauung, and one which seems almost without hope in this life. *Hiroshima* may be the most harrowing of the four to watch, but its implications are localised. The couple are transfixed in an emotional limbo, but they are special cases who represent at most a class of special cases: people who have experienced a gravely traumatic event in their lives. However, with the notion of cyclical decay and brutality, we have found a statement in *Muriel* about the human condition *per se*. We are being told that we *all*, in one way or another, will suffer and grow ugly and will fail to learn and fail to teach. Before such extreme pessimism as this, the hope that pervades *La Guerre est Finie*—where Semprun says that even though generations do not learn from each other's mistakes, certain individuals might—seems curiously inadequate.

The reason why *Muriel*, with its existential pessimism, is at odds with the other films is to be found in the general attitude of Cayrol, not Resnais. Nowhere else do we find such despair in

Resnais, and clearly the manner in which *Muriel* is directed, tautly, even perhaps coldly at times, gives no emphasis to this extreme theme. Furthermore, when he was asked by Pierre Wildenstein 'Are you an out and out pessimist or have you no faith in men?' Resnais replied as we might expect: 'Pessimist I most certainly am, but I am not prepared to be satisfied with this. There must surely be a way out. In any case, if I were nothing more than a pessimist, I wouldn't make films.' This is not the voice of *Muriel*.

Cayrol, on the other hand, has always been obsessed with the theme of the death that is at the heart of life: the Lazarean phenomenon. A former inmate of a concentration camp, he believes the camps to be an extreme image of man's living condition. 'If today the mangled body turned up by the ploughshare is kicked out of the way, if one keeps silent so as to give each individual the opportunity of being a man, it is no less true that the influence, the solicitude of the concentration camp is constantly spreading in the psyche of Europe, even of the world' (*Pour un romanesque lazaréen*). This is close to the voice of *Muriel*. For Cayrol we all encounter in a mild form the experience of camp life: the world itself is a camp, and there is nothing we can do to pull down the barbed wire or escape our guards. To live is to be possessed of a camp mentality, dead like so many Lazaruses waiting to be brought back to life by the love of God. For Cayrol is a Christian and has some hope for the future, but in *Muriel*, as it stands, this positive aspect is absent.

However, if Cayrol departs from Resnais in his extreme pessimism, there are aspects of his thought and work which are quite compatible with the director's Bergsonism. For the confused 'Lazaréens' in his novels, the world around them is a lonely and an opaque place. Things exist in space and time, forms change, but they have no meaning for Cayrol's protagonists until they succeed in reconciling their selves with their amorphous environment through the love of God. Only slowly do they learn to structure the world in terms of meanings and ideas of their own. This element of rediscovery in *Le Déménagement*, for example, although

The 'existential pessimism' of *Muriel* →

its origins and motive force are different, is compatible with, even reminiscent of, Bergson's notion of the roles of pure perceptions and pure memory in the creation of concrete perception (see p. 15). And to the extent that Cayrol's characters are presented with a meaningless world of moving forms and stubborn objects, they are in the tradition of which *La Nausée* is in mainstream, and which has its origins in Bergson's analysis of the intellect in a spatial mode.

When we have learned to structure our perceptions and through them the world, which is accomplished only with the aid of memory, we are able to leave the arena of physical space and time and capture a new *mental* chronology that orders things. In this way we conquer our loncliness among the world of objects, we become patient and humble, and we, the modern 'Lazaréens', are brought back to life. We cannot do this, however, merely by recapitulating our pasts as Bernard does: we have to re-create them. Here we have, quite explicitly, Bergson's ideas about mental time, pure and habit memory and the limitations of the spatial mode in a novelist who would appear to be closer to an existentialist tradition than anything else.

Finally Jorge Semprun, also a former inmate of a concentration camp, enables Resnais to declare himself politically without in any way moving from a general Bergsonian position. Part of the reason why this is possible is that, although Semprun seems politically far left, he does not attempt to analyse the characters or the political parties in either *La Guerre est Finie* or his novel *The Long Voyage* in Marxist terms. Anything approaching an economic interpretation of history, society or ideas would be strictly incompatible with Bergson's thought. But on the contrary, Semprun frequently satirises orthodox Marxism (but without, I suspect, rejecting Marx's class theories); and, given the move towards politics, he has much in common with Resnais. In *The Long Voyage* (1963) Manuel's conversations with 'the guy from Semur' are continually punctuated with memories of past Resistance exploits and projections of life in the future after he has survived Auschwitz—a technique which cannot but remind one of Resnais' style.

By viewing Manuel's journey in the cattle truck from different points in time, and more particularly from different stages in his emotional development, Semprun succeeds in placing this single experience in the context of his whole life. Similarly in *La Guerre est Finie*, Diego's present problems are placed in a wider context, partly by flashbacks, partly by references to the Civil War period, but perhaps more importantly by indicating the kind of man he has been through the other characters in the film. When he was very young he was like the young Leninists and Nadine, carrying plastic bombs in suitcases and possessed with ideas about revolution. Later we can guess that he became like his comrades; and when we meet him in the film he is gradually breaking away from their illusion to attain the humanity of Ramon and Marianne. Semprun's concern with memory, and the Sartrean question 'Ask him why he hasn't "made" his life, why all he has been able to do is submit to the "being" of his life. His life has always been an overwhelming "fact", a "being" outside himself which he has never been able to take possession of, to make it habitable' (*Long Voyage*), can be dealt with in certain respects in Bergsonian terms.

We must not, however, overemphasise the unity of Resnais' films. *Hiroshima* has many of those trappings of the conventional love story which are always present in Duras' work beneath the cool surface. Only in the first two films is the principle of Authorial Omniscience totally rejected. *La Guerre est Finie* is the sole optimistic achievement, and *Muriel* the solely pessimistic. In *Muriel* there is no dislocation of time or any interior monologue, while in *Marienbad* there is little else. Resnais' by now well recognisable style has been muted or emphasised as the theme and content of each film has required. The pace and visual complexity vary from the even-paced *Hiroshima* to the subtle rhythms of *Muriel*. In short, style, for Resnais, is something which is not an *a priori* concern (he is not a theorist of technique) but is a response to the demands of subject matter.

6: The Short Films

Resnais is a great director of documentaries, which, like his feature films, make up a remarkably coherent statement of his philosophical position. Since the beliefs linking his five* major shorts are in embryo those already discussed, we can avoid any further mention of the philosophy of Bergson. Instead I shall approach Resnais' themes from a rather different angle and so attempt to add a new dimension to this study.

A focal centre from which all his films radiate is the notion of personal identity. In general, the arts have been more diligent than philosophy in examining the various contexts in which we discover, defend and lose ourselves, and the modern cinema is no exception. Fellini has shown us the individual trying to rediscover his identity in childhood, creative activity and fantasy. Antonioni has made it clear that love relationships provide the crucial means by which we are to measure ourselves and that social pressure is *the* great threat to the individual. Jean-Luc Godard has analysed in considerable detail the ways in which role-playing is likely to swamp personal identity; and more recently, in *Persona*, Bergman has unfortunately approached the problem from an ontological point of view. Resnais' standpoint is rather different. He is concerned with our relationships with the external world and the inter-

---

* Omitting *Les Statues Meurent Aussi*, which I have not seen: it is still unavailable in this country owing to a ban by the French Government (lifted in 1965), and a subsequent dispute between the co-producers.

changeability of men and objects. The ubiquitous pressure of being-in-itself is, in his opinion, the greatest threat to personal identity.

Civilised society is a practical expression of some basic human needs, but might it not tend to suffocate certain impulses which it is in the interests of everyone to preserve? Some artists, for example, do not seem able to function within the confines of social organisation. They find themselves drawn to a kind of life that appears more natural (even primitive) and which allows the creative impulse complete freedom to fulfil itself. But at what cost to the artist as a human being? In the twin art films, *Gauguin* and *Van Gogh*, Resnais tries to answer this question by describing two strikingly similar creative drives.

Both painters rebelled against professions to which they were ill-fitted, and sought freedom, love and happiness through painting. Gauguin, a bank worker, 'left his house, wife, children, security and peace' and Paris 'which is a desert for a poor man' to discover first the 'savage primitive quality of Brittany' and later the beauty of Tahiti and its people. Van Gogh, the pastor of Neumen, who 'preached badly, the violence of his faith drove away the believers,' tried to express his love of man in other ways. He soon tired of painting Holland and Paris, 'he felt the selfishness of the huge town weigh on him' and 'dreamed of other deeper joys, of a different light,' which he found at Arles and Saint Rémy. So both men cut themselves off from normal human society and indulged to the full their desire to paint. And the result? On the one hand, works of genius; on the other, solitude and disease for Gauguin; madness and suicide for Van Gogh. In nature, free from the drabness and restrictions of city life, they found the beauty and colour for which they had always longed. Yet eventually they were destroyed by their monomania. Their freedom was too total; nature was too strong for their imaginations to keep on forcing it into the confines of a painting.

Gauguin, 'exhausted by the unremitting struggle I had undertaken,' saddened by the 'superstitious fears emanating from the forces of unknown nature' which plagued the Tahitians, and debilitated by disease, became incapable of doing any sustained

A sequence from *Van Gogh* (*frame enlargements*) →

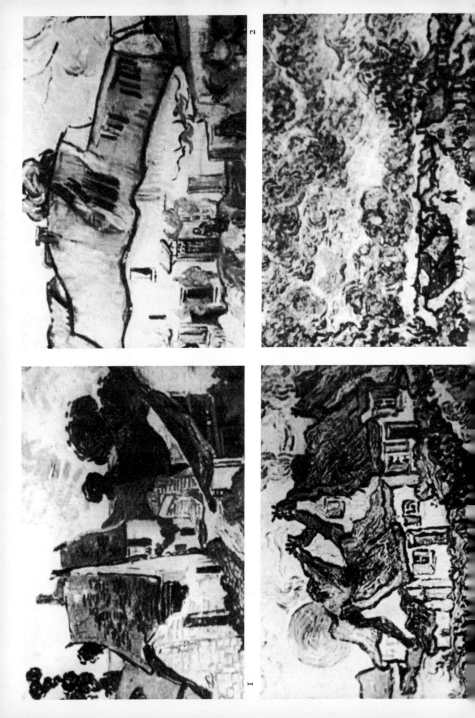

1

2

5

6

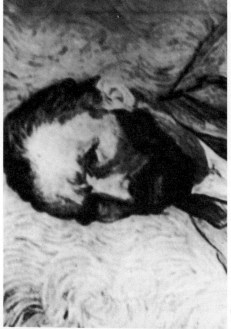

7

8

work. Without family or friends to sustain him, he realised that 'death was infinitely preferable' to such emptiness. He had sacrificed everything to his painting, choosing nature in preference to human beings, and inevitably he died a lonely man whose thoughts returned to 'an imaginary scene of Brittany in the snow,' but who could merely paint yet another self-portrait on the morning of his death. The primitive life of Tahiti with all its beauty was an inadequate substitute for civilised society.

Similarly, Van Gogh, who 'gazed intensely, with the same love, at both human beings and objects,' 'had long since accepted renouncing everything but not his work.' Cut off from the security of human contact, 'he felt the appearance of things escaping him,' and Sartrean 'Nature struck him in the face.' 'The universe which he discovered appeared measureless, fathomless.' The physical world bombarded him with stimuli too powerful for his senses to receive or for his imagination to organise. He became ill and 'from now on a fire burned in him and deprived him of all his being.' His identity was swallowed up by Nature. Unable to continue the struggle to subdue the pressure of nature to the demands of art, he chose the peace of death.

The conclusion of these two shorts is a dilemma. Men cannot live alone, confronting Nature, without losing their identities, but for men such as Van Gogh and Gauguin there seems little alternative. In the Van Gogh film, paintings are selected to show the gradual blurring of the painter's sense of self-definition. We see how the background colours, the vivid ochres of some later paintings submerge all detail, particularly human figures. Great yellow canvasses of cornfields, sunflowers, and above all, the sun itself, hammer the brain. Van Gogh had lost all identity in a wild flow of colour. United in this loss were genius and tragedy. Resnais even suggests that Van Gogh's suicide was compelled by the same kind of physical pressure caused by the sun's glare that made Camus' Meursault tighten his finger on the gun which caused the death of the Arab. This interpretation, suggested by repeated close-ups of the sun which bludgeon one's senses, seems incompatible with the script's emphasis on the painter's free choice of death.

Thus only within society can men control objects to their own ends, because human society represents the success of man in organising and dominating the physical world. Social institutions and relationships are designed to protect us from the disorder, the randomness of our environments. In *Le Chant du Styrène*, we are told in a quotation from Victor Hugo that 'Man expects matter to serve him,' and the film proceeds to show us in detail how this expectation is fulfilled. But even this factual documentary is not without malicious implications. The title itself, and the sight of the polystyrene writhing its way through various processes as if it had a life of its own, hint that we are only just in control. Indeed, the very knowledge which enabled us to use Nature for our advantage came by accident, not design.

We can even become dependent on the physical objects we use within society. Resnais illustrates this danger in *Toute la Mémoire du Monde*, and introduces for the first time his central theme, the nature of memory. Our memories are short so we write books which we store in libraries. And, as our knowledge increases, so the piles of books grow at a terrifying rate until we are in peril of being submerged by the sheer number of words, lost among the innumerable shelves of books. In order to safeguard our freedom, we design our libraries like fortresses in which 'this mass of writings, this pile of words is imprisoned.' Beside 'this gigantic memory' of the Bibliothèque Nationale, our own memories are insignificant, and while ours can be distorted by time, these books are permanent, protected by their solidity and by the care we take of them. To complete our ruin we have used our intelligence to 'sort them, analyse them, classify and number them,' for 'without catalogues, this fortress would be like a country without roads.' And because the collection is continually growing, we have become slaves to the demands of the catalogue: to our intellects. In the service of this swelling bulk, 'disciplines have had to be invented which time has converted into laws.'

Yet not only do these volumes threaten us with their bulk, they take from us our humanity. While we become 'paper eating insects,' the books themselves are treated with care comparable to that bestowed on the most delicate invalid. 'These riches must be preserved, that is why the air is controlled and the atmosphere regulated. Machinery . . . maintains a constant temperature, suitable for paper, leather and parchment. Day and night there is constant supervision, whatever the cost, destruction must be averted.* A subtle ointment preserves the bindings. Holes made by insects are sealed off. Thin pages are mounted. The books are inoculated, given covers.' They are anthropomorphised; perhaps in their new role they will from their vast store of information render up to one of their readers 'the fragments of a single secret . . . which is called happiness.'

Toute la Mémoire du Monde is written and directed as a personification. Books take on human qualities, capable of being aggressive, of being imprisoned or nursed and of having identities which men cherish as they would those of personal friends. Resnais takes us a further move from reality with the opening shot of the camera, looking like a three-eyed robot, and the microphone which dips down when the narrator is to speak. We are in the hands of machines which will show us what we are to see and enable us to hear what we are to be told. And not only the audience is dependent upon these objects; so are Resnais and his crew. The style and implications of this overture are reminiscent of certain of Samuel Beckett's stage devices.

A series of tracking shots establishes the sheer volume of books in the Bibliothèque and its similarity to a great underground prison with its lifts, grills, locks and keys. Within this environment a short biography is recounted. The biography of a travel book which is bought, stamped, catalogued, given an identity sheet and a place on the shelves. And like all good biographies, it presents us with a crucial event in the subject's 'life'. Someone has ordered the book, and we see it make its journey from the lower depths to

---

* This passage is worth quoting in full for the contrast it provides with the treatment of human beings in *Nuit et Brouillard*. For the Jews there was constant supervision to *facilitate* destruction. There was 'subtle ointment' too, one to cure all ills. The air was controlled and there were inoculations, but for another purpose entirely.

the reading room. It has justified its purchase: it has fulfilled its social duty. Finally the dome of the library itself is anthropomorphised. An image of the human brain is contracted to the size of the dome, and later we see this huge head from the inside, containing the world's memory.

In Resnais' finest short film, *Nuit et Brouillard*, the idea that human beings and physical objects are interchangeable is given extended treatment and blended with two other themes: the nature of appearance and reality, and the effect of the passage of time on human memory.

Twenty years have elapsed since American troops liberated Auschwitz and the outside world was presented for the first time with the full horror of the 'final solution'. Except for stretches of barbed wire and a few broken-down buildings, the camp looks like a typical stretch of Polish countryside. 'Weeds have grown where prisoners walked,' and however hard we try to imagine the pain and misery of life there, we cannot independently recollect it, and 'only the husk and the shade remain.' Statistics do not carry the burden of personal tragedy. So the grass grows and the river, 'a water as sluggish as our memory,' flows away. We forget too easily. The present Auschwitz at which we call during our holidays for a guided tour seems more real than when it was functional. Resnais underlines this fact by shooting the camp as it is today in colour, which is contrasted with the blurred, scratchy newsreels and photographs of the past. Even films age.

The appearance of the camps was an ironic comment on their morality. Like the language used by the SS, they were a euphemism. For the purposes of extermination (what can that word alone conjure?), the Nazis built apparently social units which, as all good communities should, contained hospitals with up-to-date operating theatres, factories which provided its people with work, a good train service, shower-baths and even brothels. But in these hospitals the sick were allowed to starve to death and all ills were treated with the same ointment. The purpose of these operating theatres was not to alleviate suffering. In the factories not only value was surplus, and the train service never took people back home after their visits. There was the irony of a prison within a city which is itself a prison. And perhaps the supreme irony: in the midst of this society which has 'developed the image of terror,' rests a great symbol of culture: Goethe's oak. Finally, to round off the illusion, the commandant and his family act out the fantasy that the camp does not exist at all.

What of the people who live in this society? They have long since become things. The Nazis themselves, as we have seen them at the Nuremberg rallies, are models of *mechanical* precision. The Kapos and orderlies have the faces of brutes. As for the prisoners, they are treated as objects. They are categorised, stamped, graded and tattooed just like the books in *Toute la Mémoire*, except that unlike the books, no one takes any trouble to preserve them. Camp inmates are graded to facilitate the business of extermination. And eventually they *become* objects. Their hair is woven into cloth, their bodies are rendered down for soap and their bones are used to make chemical fertilisers. 'With typical German thoroughness nothing is wasted.' This is the final stage in the reduction of man to a commodity (beyond even the comprehension of Marx), an object of intelligence no longer capable of evoking any kind of emotional response. As we watch the film, it is difficult to make any distinction between the grotesque parodies of human beings bulldozed into a lime-pit and the rooms full of crutches, spectacles and hair. If anything, the latter possess more human associations, and overwhelm us with the personal misery they represent, while the corpses merely make us recoil with disgust: a far more manageable response.

However, if the passage of time has made us forgetful, perhaps it has also made us able to view the horror with some kind of objectivity. Can we say, even now, why it happened? No one will admit responsibility, no one feels ashamed. But is it appropriate to particularise responsibility? Cayrol thinks not. 'Are their faces really so different from ours?' he asks, and ends on a typical note of utter pessimism, criticising 'those with hope, as if there is a cure for the scourge of these camps.'

Nuit et Brouillard is an exercise in artistic restraint. Resnais allows actual photographs and films to speak for him: in the few scenes he shot specially for the film, points are made visually, and, in Cayrol's script, with infinite sadness rather than anger. A shot of the outside of the camp hospital bathed in red light says all that needs to be said about its purpose. The newsreel of Himmler and his staff jocularly suggesting improvements to a design of the camps requires no comment and is given none. The result is an unbearably painful film which at no point resorts to sensationalism or facile judgements. Resnais has realised that the old films speak for themselves and that the director has no need to emphasise them by direct statement. Instead, by visual contrasts and by juxtaposing scenes of horror with films of clean, disciplined Nazis and shots of the tranquillity of Auschwitz today, he organises his material into a powerful whole. Such restraint makes *Nuit et Brouillard* unique among films about the camps: it succeeds in treating its subject with dignity.

While the concentration camps represent a tragedy that affected people of many countries, a fact which Resnais acknowledges by enumerating the varied styles of camp architecture, Guernica was a Spanish tragedy. Picasso's painting contains notable Spanish imagery: the bull, the agonised horse's head, which are frequently exploited by Resnais. And Paul Eluard's poem which comprises most of the script is remarkably Spanish in style. Such lines as 'They have made you pay with the bread of your life. They have made you pay with the sky, the earth, the water, the sleep of your life' are typical. The Lorcan idea of *la muerte* is referred to: 'You did not expect death. Fear and the courage to live and die. Death so difficult and so easy.' Concisely Eluard captures the gratuitous savagery of the air raid, the aim of which 'was to test the combined effects of high explosive and incendiary bombs on a civilian population,' with lines such as 'The machine-gun bullets played with the children, better than the wind,' and 'By fire and steel Man was hollowed out like a mine.' The raid was utterly undiscriminating in fact, and in the sight of God: 'The women, the children, had the same pink cheeks in His eyes.'

We have seen what happens when men cut themselves off from

A sequence from *Guernica* (*frame enlargements*) →

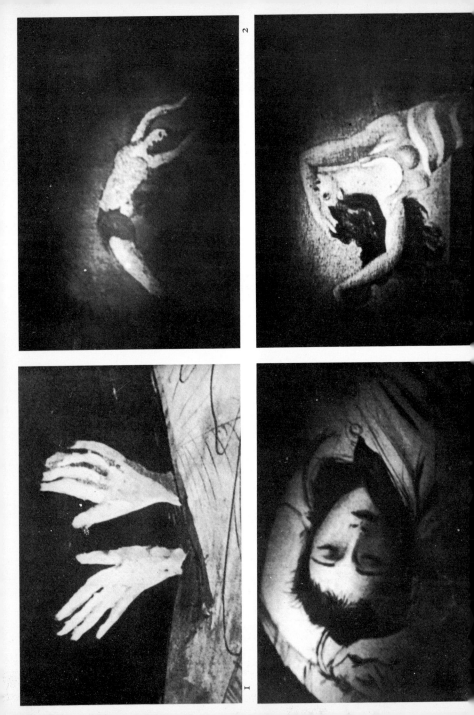

5

6

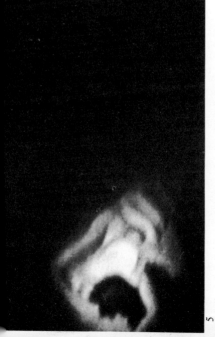

7

8

society (*Van Gogh* and *Gauguin*), and how men can control (*Le Chant du Styrène*) and be controlled (*Toute la Mémoire du Monde*) by objects even within society. Then in *Nuit et Brouillard* we were given a case of men creating a grotesque society in which men are nothing more than objects; and now, in *Guernica*, we see the horror which results when one society treats another as an object. The Nazis tested their air power on Guernica as nonchalantly as we test our nuclear weapons in the desert. The people of that town were of no more importance to the Nazis than are grains of sand to us.

But what was the attitude of the rest of the world at the time? 'We read it all in the papers, drinking our coffee: somewhere in Europe a legion of assassins were crushing a human ant-heap,' and 'In boots and helmets, well-behaved, good-looking fellows, the aviators dropped their bombs.' Distance in space reduced the disaster for the rest of the world in 1937, as distance in time does for us today. To men living twenty years later 'Guernica has only historical and sentimental value.' And even if we were not indifferent, what could we do? How could we 'hold back death' or 'Explain to a mother the death of her child?'

If there is a message in the film, it is that war, which by definition compels man to treat man as an object, is the ultimate horror. One fact is certain, 'There is only one night, and it is that of war, elder sister of poverty and daughter of revolting, hideous death,' and Picasso says this better than we can. War which degrades man to the level of the inanimate must be avoided. 'My brothers, here you are transformed to carrion, to broken skeletons. The earth turns in your orbits. You are a rotted desert, and death has broken the balance of time.'

Picasso's painting consists of a series of images of individual agony; it makes no reference to the air attack itself, so Resnais has to rely on Eluard's script to provide the wider military context. By remaining completely within the painting and by blacking out the frame of the film, when he concentrates on Picasso's sculptured reliefs Resnais does not allow the audience any deliverance from the intensity of these images. At times he anticipates his later technique of over-exposing certain scenes, when he fills the screen with the luminosity of great pale faces and the naked light bulb. This enables him to exploit an ambiguity in the painting which, at times, suggests the interrogation cell, and at others, the blinding light of explosions which twist and mutilate human faces and bodies. In either case, the result is something unreal to most of our personal experience.

The short films express a dilemma in very pessimistic terms which the feature films are to wrestle with and give several hypothetical solutions to. They present a *mise en scène* which the longer films are to people with appropriate characters. As usual in Resnais' work, there is a perfect congruity of the various elements out of which they are constructed.

Claude Rich and Olga Georges-Picot in *Je t'aime, Je t'aime* →

Filmography

We are extremely grateful to *l'Avant-Scène du Cinéma* for permission to reprint credits of and information about films not available in England or U.S.A.

(See issues numbers 1, 52 and in particular 61–62, a special double issue devoted exclusively to Alain Resnais and containing an invaluable bio-filmography by Francis Lacassin.)

Alain Resnais

Born Vannes, Brittany, 3 June 1922

Studied at the college of Saint-François-Xavier, Vannes

1936	Made several 8 mm films
1940–42	Studied acting under René Simon
1943–45	Studied at I.D.H.E.C. (course uncompleted)
1945	Military service with the occupation army in Germany and Austria, where he was a member of a travelling theatrical company, Les Arlinquins
	Lighting cameraman on *Le Sommeil d'Albertine* (also known as *Les Yeux d'Albertine*, Jean Leduc)
1947	Lighting cameraman on an advertising film *Transfo Transforme l'Energie du Pyrium* (Remo Forlani)
	Assistant director and assistant editor on *Paris 1900* (Nicole Védrès)
1948	Lighting cameraman and editor on a television film *Jean Effel*
1949	Editor (with Remo Forlani) on *La Tournée Boussac en Afrique Noire*
	Special effects director on *Versailles et ses Fantômes* (Jean Béranger)
1952	Editor on *Saint-Tropez, Devoir de Vacances* (Paul Paviot)
1953	Editor on *Aux Frontières de l'Homme* (Nicole Védrès, Jean Rostand)
1955	Editor on *La Pointe Courte* (Agnès Varda)
1957	Editor and technical adviser on *Broadway by Light* (William Klein)
	Co-editor on *L'Oeil du Maître* (Jacques Doniol-Valcroze)

Resnais is Vice-President of the Centre d'Etude des Littératures d'Expression Graphique, and a member of the editorial board of *Giff-Wiff*, a magazine devoted to the documentation of the comic-strip.

Features

Ouvert pour cause d'Inventaire (1946)

Director   Alain Resnais
Danièle Delorme, Nadine Alari, Pierre Trebaud, and (briefly) Gérard Philipe.

Shot in 16 mm, this was Resnais' first feature length film. There are no copies still in existence.

Un Dimanche tous Ensemble (1956)

Producer   Pierre Braunberger
Director   Alain Resnais
Script   Remo Forlani

Intended as a 35 mm feature film about a group of adolescents wandering around Paris one Sunday. Although Forlani had already advanced some money for the film, Resnais abandoned the project because he felt incapable of making the film along the lines originally envisaged: cinéma vérité techniques; the camera concealed in the back of a lorry; a large degree of improvisation.

L'Ile Noire (1957)

Production Company   Les Films du Matin
Producer   Eugénie Hélisse
Director   Alain Resnais
Script   Remo Forlani. Based on the Tintin story by Hergé

This was to have been a 35 mm feature length film in colour. Resnais and Forlani envisaged using extremely artificial and stylised décors, with actors wearing masks designed by Hergé. The project was abandoned, but taken up in a different form by the producer-scriptwriter André Barret, who commissioned Forlani to adapt *Tintin et le Mystère de la Toison d'or*, directed by Jean-Jacques Vierne in 1961.

Hiroshima, Mon Amour (1959)

Production Company	Argos Films/Como Films (Paris)/Daieï (Tokyo)/Pathé Overseas
Executive Producer	Samy Halfon
Production Managers	Sacha Kamenka, Shirakawa Takeo
Director	Alain Resnais
Assistant Directors	T. Andréfouet, J.-P. Léon, R. Guyonnet, I. Shirai, Itoi, Hara
Script	Marguerite Duras
Literary Adviser	Gérard Jarlot
Dialogue	Marguerite Duras
Directors of Photography	Sacha Vierny (France), Michio Takahashi (Japan)
Camera Operators	Pierre Goupil, Watanabe, Ioda
Editors	Henri Colpi, Jasmine Chasney, Anne Sarraute
Art Directors	Esaka, Mayo, Petri
Music	Giovanni Fusco, Georges Delerue (also two records of Japanese music for the procession and the juke-box)
Costumes	Gérard Collery
Sound	Pierre Calvet, Yamamoto, René Renault

Emmanuèle Riva (*She*), Eiji Okada (*He*), Bernard Fresson (*The German*), Stella Dassas (*The Mother*), Pierre Barbaud (*The Father*).

Filmed on location in Hiroshima and Nevers; Japanese interiors shot in Tokyo, French interiors at the Studios Paris; September–December 1958. First shown at the Cannes Film Festival (out of competition), 8 May 1959; Paris, 10 June 1959; G.B., 7 January 1960; U.S.A., May 1960. Running time, 91 mins. (88 mins. in U.S.A.).
Distributors: Cocinor (France), Gala (G.B.), Zenith (U.S.A.).

L'Année Dernière à Marienbad (1961)

Production Company	Terra-Film/Société Nouvelle des Films Cormoran/Précitel/Como-Films/Les Films Tamara/Cinetel/Silver Films (Paris)/Cineriz (Rome)
Producers	Pierre Courau (Précitel), Raymond Froment (Terra-Film)
Production Manager	Léon Sanz
Director	Alain Resnais
Assistant Director	Jean Léon
Script	Alain Robbe-Grillet
Director of Photography	Sacha Vierny (Dyaliscope)
Camera Operator	Philippe Brun
Editors	Henri Colpi, Jasmine Chasney
Art Director	Jacques Saulnier
Set Decorators	Georges Glon, André Piltant, Jean-Jacques Fabre
Music	Francis Seyrig
Musical Director	André Girard
Organist	Marie Louise
Costumes	Delphine Seyrig's two 'feather' costumes by Bernard Evein; her other dresses by Chanel
Titles	Jean Fouchet
Sound	Guy Villette
Sound Recordists	Jean-Claude Marchetti, René Renault, Jean Nény, Robert Cambourakis

Delphine Seyrig (*A*), Giorgio Albertazzi (*X*), Sacha Pitoëff (*M*), Françoise Bertin, Luce Garcia-Ville, Héléna Kornel, Françoise Spira, Karin Toeche-Mittler, Pierre Barbaud, Wilhelm Von Deek, Jean Lanier, Gérard Lorin, Davide Montemuri, Gilles Quéant, Gabriel Werner.

Filmed on location in Munich in various châteaux including Nymphenburg and Schleissheim, and in the Photosonor Studios in Paris; September–November 1960. First shown at the Venice Film Festival, 29 August 1961; Paris, 29 September 1961; G.B., 22 February 1962; U.S.A., 7 March 1962. Running time, 94 mins.

Distributors: Cocinor (France), Compton-Cameo/Sebricon (G.B.), Astor (U.S.A.).

U.S./G.B. title: LAST YEAR IN MARIENBAD.

Resnais directing his episode in *Far from Vietnam* →

Muriel, ou le Temps d'un Retour (1963)

Production Company	Argos Films/Alpha Productions/Eclair/ Films de la Pléiade (Paris)/Dear Film (Rome)
Producer	Anatole Dauman
Production Manager	Philippe Dussart
Director	Alain Resnais
Assistant Director	Jean Léon
Script	Jean Cayrol
Director of Photography	Sacha Vierny
Colour Process	Eastman Colour
Camera Operator	Philippe Brun
Editors	Kenout Peltier, Eric Pluet
Art Director	Jacques Saulnier
Music	Hans Werner Henze
Singer	Rita Streich
Song 'Déjà'	Paul Colline, Paul Maye
Titles	Jan Lenica
Sound	Antoine Bonfanti

Delphine Seyrig (*Hélène Aughain*), Jean-Pierre Kérien (*Alphonse Noyard*), Nita Klein (*Françoise*), Jean-Baptiste Thierrée (*Bernard*), Claude Sainval (*Roland de Smoke*), Jean Champion (*Ernest*), Laurence Badie (*Claudie*), Martine Vatel (*Marie-Do*), Philippe Laudenbach (*Robert*), Jean Dasté (*Man with the Goat*), Robert Bordenave (*The Croupier*), Gaston Joly (*Antoine, the tailor*), Catherine de Seynes (*Angèle, the tailor's wife*), Julien Verdier (*The Stableman*), Gérard Lorin, Françoise Bertin, Wanda Kérien, Jean-Jacques Lagarde.

Filmed on location at Boulogne-sur-mer, and at the Studios Du Mont, Epinay-sur-Seine; November 1962–January 1963. First shown in Paris, 24 July 1963; G.B., 19 March 1964 (previously at London Film Festival, 22 October 1963); U.S.A., November 1963 (previously at New York Film Festival, 18 September 1963). Running time, 116 mins.

Distributors: United Artists (France, G.B. and U.S.A.).

La Guerre est Finie (1966)

Production Company	Sofracima (Paris)/Europa-Film (Stockholm)
Production Manager	Alain Queffeléan

Director	Alain Resnais
Assistant Director	Jean Léon, Florence Malraux
Script	Jorge Semprun
Director of Photography	Sacha Vierny
Camera Operator	Philippe Brun
Editor	Eric Pluet
Art Director	Jacques Saulnier
Music	Giovanni Fusco
Sound	Antoine Bonfanti
Narrator	Jorge Semprun

Yves Montand (*Diego Mora*), Ingrid Thulin (*Marianne*), Geneviève Bujold (*Nadine Sallanches*), Dominique Rozan (*Jude*), Françoise Bertin (*Carmen*), Michel Piccoli (*Customs Inspector*), Paul Crauchet (*Roberto*), Gérard Séty (*Bill*), Jean Bouise (*Ramon*), Anouk Ferjac (*Madame Jude*), Yvette Etiévant (*Yvette*), Jean Dasté (*The Chief*), Annie Fargue (*Agnès*), Gérard Lartigau (*Head of students' revolutionary group*), Jacques Rispal (*Manolo*), Jean-François Rémi (*Juan*), Pierre Leproux (*Maker of forged papers*), Marie Mergey (*Madame Lopez*), Marcel Cuvelier (*Inspector Chardin*), Roland Monod (*Antoine*), Bernard Fresson (*Sarlat*), Laurence Badie (*Bernadette Pluvier*), José-María Flotats (*Miguel*), Catherine de Seynes (*Jeanine*), Claire Duhamel (*Traveller*), Jean Larroquette (*Student*), Martine Vatel (*Student*), R.-J. Chauffard (*Tramp*), Antoine Vitez (*Air France employee*), Jacques Robnard (*Pierrot*), Paillette (*Old Woman*), Jacques Wallet (*Security Policeman*), Pierre Decazes (*Railway worker*), Jean Bolo (*Policeman*), Pierre Barbaud (*A Client*).

Filmed on location in Stockholm and Paris; August–November 1965. First shown at the Cannes Festival (out of competition), 9 May 1966; Paris, 11 May 1966; G.B., 1 August 1966; U.S.A., January 1967 (previously at New York Film Festival, 22 September 1966). Running time, 121 mins.

Distributors: Cocinor (France), Gala (G.B.), Brandon Films (U.S.A.). G.B. title: THE WAR IS OVER.

Loin du Viêt-Nam (1967)

Production Company	Slon
Directors	Alain Resnais, William Klein, Joris Ivens, Agnès Varda, Claude Lelouch, Jean-Luc Godard

Organisers	Jacqueline Meppiel, Andrea Haran
Principal Collaborators	Michèle Ray, Roger Pic, K. S. Karol, Marceline Loridan, François Maspero, Chris Marker, Jacques Sternberg, Jean Lacoutre, Willy Kurant, Jean Bosty, Kieu Tham, Denis Clairval, Ghislain Cloquet, Bernard Zitzerman, Alain Levent, Théo Robichet, Antoine Bonfanti, Harold Maury, Claire Grunstein, Alain Franchet, Didier Beaudet, Florence Malraux, Marie-Louise Guinet, Roger de Menestrol, Ragnar, Jean Ravel, Colette Leloup, Eric Pluet, Albert Jurgenson, Ethel Blum, Michèle Bouder, Christian Quinson, Jean Larivière, Maurice Carrel, Bernard Fresson, Karen Blanguernon, Anne Bellec, Valérie Mayoux
Colour Process	Eastman Colour (in part only)

First shown at the Montreal Film Festival, August 1967; G.B., 28 December 1967 (previously at London Film Festival, 29 November 1967); U.S.A., New York Film Festival, 30 September 1967; France, 13 December 1967 (previously at Besançon before an audience of Trade Union Members, 18 October 1967). Running time, 115 mins.

Distributors: Films 13 (France), Contemporary (G.B.).

U.S./G.B. title: FAR FROM VIETNAM.

Je t'Aime, Je t'Aime (1968)

Production Company	Parc Film—Fox Europa
Producer	Mag Bodard
Production Manager	Philippe Dussart
Director	Alain Resnais
Assistant Directors	Jean Lefèvre, Florence Malraux
Script	Jacques Sternberg
Adaptation and Dialogue	Alain Resnais, Jacques Sternberg
Director of Photography	Jean Boffety
Colour Process	Eastman Colour
Art Director	Jacques Dugied
Sound	Antoine Bonfanti

Claude Rich (*Claude Ridder*), Olga Georges-Picot (*Catrine*), Anouk Ferjac (*Wiana*), Van Doude (*Rouffers*), Dominique Rozan (*Dr Haesserts*), Yves Kerboul (*Xammers*), Ray Verhaege (*Goofers, Technician A*), Pierre Barbaud (*Levino, Technician B*), Alain Mac Moy (*Moyens*), Vania Vilers (*Jacques Rheuys*), Georges Jamin (*Clinical Surgeon*), Carla Marlier (*Nicole*), Marie-Blanche Vergne (*Young Woman in Tram*), Claire Duhamel (*Ridder's Secretary*), Annie Bertin (*Young Mother*), Hélène Callot (*Nurse*), Bernard Valdeneige (*First Ad. Man*), Jean Martin (*Second Ad. Man*), Alan Adair (*Inspector*), Jean-Louis Richard (*Friend in Restaurant Car*), M. Floquet (*Mr Grabet*), Pierre Motte (*Mr Lambert*), Billy Farbender (*Employee*), Jean Pierre (*Editor*), Michèle Blondel (*Woman Employee*).

Filmed on location in Nice, Brussels, and Paris.

Distributors: Fox (France, G.B., U.S.A.).

Resnais has for some time now been hoping to make a 70 mm colour film called *Les Aventures d'Harry Dickson*, based on the novels by Jean Ray. A script was written and a shortened version (140 mins.) prepared at the request of Anatole Dauman and Athos Films; but as yet nothing definite has come of this project.

Shorts

Fantômas (1936)

Director	Alain Resnais
Script	Based on the novels by Pierre Souvestre and Marcel Allain

An 8 mm short. The cast consisted of Vannes school-children.

L'Aventure de Guy (1936)

Director	Alain Resnais
Script	Gaston Modot
Director of Photography	Alain Resnais
Editor	Alain Resnais

A 16 mm short. The script was presumably one of the many that Modot published in a review for amateur cinéastes; the title is Resnais' own.

Schéma d'une Identification (1946)

Director   Alain Resnais

A 16 mm silent film featuring Gérard Philipe and François Chaumette. According to Resnais, all copies of the film have been lost.

In 1947 Resnais directed a series of 16 mm shorts about various painters. The titles in this series are:

Visite à Lucien Coutaud
(This film was shown on French television in 1962)
Visite à Félix Labisse
Visite à Hans Hartung
Visite à César Domela
Visite à Oscar Dominguez
Portrait de Henri Goetz
Journée Naturelle (also titled *Visite à Max Ernst*). In colour.

La Bague (1947)

Director   Alain Resnais

A 16 mm mime-drama featuring Marcel Marceau.

L'Alcool Tue (1947)

Production Company	Les Films de la Roue
Producers	Christiane Renty, Paul Renty
Director	Alain Resnais (under the pseudonym of Alzin Rezarail)
Script	Remo Forlani, Roland Dubillard
Text	Alzin Rezarail [Alain Resnais]
Director of Photography	Alzin Rezarail [Alain Resnais]
Editor	Alzin Rezarail [Alain Resnais]
Sound	Alain Resnais (from gramophone records)

Roland Dubillard, Remo Forlani, Robert Mendigal (*The Workmen*), Claude Charpentier (*The Priest*), Christiane Renty, Colette Renty (*The Women*), Paul Renty (*The Foreman*).

Filmed in two days on location in a quarry near Meaux (Seine et Marne).

A 16 mm short fantasy involving some drunken workmen and a proselytising priest.

Campagne Première (1947)

Production Company	Les Films de la Roue
Director	Alain Resnais
Script	Remo Forlani
Director of Photography	Alain Resnais
Editor	Alain Resnais

Shot in 16 mm, *Campagne Première* was to have been a medium length 'reportage' about the painters living on the Rue Campagne-Première. The project was definitively abandoned when Forlani left Paris to do his Military Service, and Resnais incorporated it into his *Visites* series.

In 1947, Resnais made two commercials (in colour) for Nestlé's Milk. These films have identical titles and identical credits:

Le Lait Nestlé (1947)

Production Company	l'Agence A.B.C.
Directors	Remo Forlani, Fernand Marzelle, Alain Resnais
Script	Remo Forlani, Fernand Marzelle, Alain Resnais
Director of Photography	Alain Resnais
Editor	Alain Resnais

Filmed in the maternity hospital at Montmorency. Running time, 1 min.

Les Jardins de Paris (1948)

Production Company	Les Films de la Roue
Producers	Christiane Renty, Paul Renty
Director	Alain Resnais. The sequence in the *Jardin des Plantes* was directed by André Bazin
Assistant Director	Colette Renty

| Director of Photography | Alain Resnais, assisted by Colette Renty |
| Editor | Alain Resnais, assisted by Colette Renty |

An unfinished documentary, filmed in several public parks in Paris and on the roof of the Louvre.

Châteaux de France (1948)

Production Company	Ciné-Gimm
Director	Alain Resnais
Script	Alain Resnais
Director of Photography	Alain Resnais
Colour Process	Kodachrome
Editor	Alain Resnais

Shot in 16 mm, the film is a stills montage of the *châteaux touristiques*. To make it, Resnais cycled alone around France, carrying the necessary equipment on his back.

Van Gogh (1948)

Producer	Pierre Braunberger
Production Manager	Claude Hauser
Director	Alain Resnais
Script	Robert Hessens, Gaston Diehl
Director of Photography and Special Effects	Henri Ferrand
Editor	Alain Resnais
Music	Jacques Besse
Sound	Studio Saint-Maurice
Commentary	Gaston Diehl
Narrator	Claude Dauphin

The 16 mm version of this film, made in 1947 for 'Les Amis de l'Art', was entirely re-made by Resnais in 35 mm at the request of Pierre Braunberger. *Van Gogh* was the first of Resnais' films to be professionally commissioned.

First shown in Paris, May 1948; G.B., October 1950; U.S.A., January 1950. Running time, 20 mins. (18 mins. in U.S.A.).

Distributors: Panthéon (les Films de la Pléiade) (France), French Institute (G.B.), Canton-Weiner (U.S.A.).

Malfray (1948)

Directors	Alain Resnais, Robert Hessens
Script	Gaston Diehl, Robert Hessens
Music	Pierre Barbaud

In 16 mm.

Gauguin (1950)

Production Company	Panthéon (Paris)
Producer	Pierre Braunberger
Director	Alain Resnais
Script	Gaston Diehl
Director of Photography and Special Effects	Henri Ferrand
Editor	Alain Resnais
Music	Darius Milhaud
Commentary	Taken from the letters of Paul Gauguin
Narrator	Jean Servais

First shown in Paris, June 1951. Running time, 11 mins.
Distributors: Panthéon (France), French Institute (G.B.).

Guernica (1950)

Production Company	Panthéon
Producer	Pierre Braunberger
Production Manager	Claude Hauser
Directors	Alain Resnais, Robert Hessens
Script	Robert Hessens
Director of Photography and Special Effects	Henri Ferrand
Camera Operators	André Dumaître, W. Novik
Editor	Alain Resnais
Music	Guy Bernard

Musical Director	Marc Vaubourgoin
Sound	Pierre-Louis Calvet
Text	Paul Eluard
Narrators	Maria Casarès, Jacques Pruvost

First shown in Paris, June 1950. Running time, 12 mins.
Distributors: Films de la Pléiade (France), French Institute (G.B.).

Les Statues Meurent Aussi (1950–1953)

Production Company	Présence Africaine/Tadié-Cinéma
Directors	Alain Resnais, Chris Marker
Script	Alain Resnais, Chris Marker
Director of Photography	Ghislain Cloquet
Editor	Alain Resnais
Music	Guy Bernard
Sound	Studio Marignan
Commentary	Alain Resnais, Chris Marker
Narrator	Jean Negroni

Started in 1950 at the request of Présence Africaine, the film was completed, after an interruption, in 1953. Its theme is the decline of Negro art as a result of contact with Western civilisation. It was banned by the French Censor until 1965, and as a result of a dispute between its co-producers it has still not been shown to the general public, although it was shown at the Cannes Film Festival in 1953. Running time, 30 mins.
Distributors: Tadié (France) own the French rights.

Nuit et Brouillard (1955)

Production Company	Argos Films/Como Films
Production Manager	Edouard Muszka
Director	Alain Resnais
Assistant Director	André Heinrich
Directors of Photography	Ghislain Cloquet, Sacha Vierny
Colour Process	Eastman Colour (in part only)
Editors	Henri Colpi, Jasmine Chasney
Historical Advisers	Henri Michel, Olga Wormser

Music	Hanns Eisler
Commentary	Jean Cayrol
Narrator	Michel Bouquet

First shown in Paris, 16 May 1956 (previously shown at the Cannes Film Festival out of competition, 8 May 1956); G.B., 14 February 1960 (previously at the National Film Theatre, 15 December 1956). Running time, 31 mins.

Distributors: Argos Films (France), Gala (G.B.), Contemporary (U.S.A.).

Toute la Mémoire du Monde (1956)

Production Company	Les Films de la Pléiade
Producer	Pierre Braunberger
Director	Alain Resnais
Script	Remo Forlani
Director of Photography	Ghislain Cloquet
Editor	Alain Resnais
Music	Maurice Jarre
Musical Director	Georges Delerue
Sound	Studio Marignan
Commentary	Remo Forlani
Narrator	Jacques Dumesnil

'With the collaboration of': Gérard Willemetz, Pierre Goupil, Anne Sarraute, Roger Fleytoux, Claude Joudioux, Jean Cayrol, André Goefers, Jean-Charles Lauthe, Chris and Magic Marker, Phil Davis, Robert Rendigal, Giuletta Caput, Claudine Merlin, Dominique Raoul Duval, Chester Gould, Denis York, Benigne Caceres, Agnès Varda, Monique Le Porrier, Paulette Borker, André Heinrich, Mme. Searle, Marie-Claire Pasquier, François-Régis Bastide, Joseph Rovan. [These credits are something of an in-joke; the more obvious of them refer to extremely brief appearances intended principally to amuse the makers of the film.]

Filmed in and on the Bibliothèque Nationale in Paris. Running time, 22 mins.

Distributors: Films de la Pléiade (France), French Institute (G.B.).

In 1957 Bernard Quillon, a mutual friend of Resnais and Forlani, envisaged founding a production company. At Resnais' suggestion, he decided to call it Protéa-Films, a name which, while paying tribute to Victorin Jasset, appealed to them because of its vague Romantic overtones. The first work of this still-born company was to have been a series of forty black and white, 16 mm technical films whose title and subject matter were to be:

L'Organisation du Travail (1957)

Production Company	Protéa-Films
Producer	Bernard Quillon
Director	Alain Resnais
Script	Remo Forlani, as adviser to Monsieur de Monesse and Monsieur de Mouy

From this abandoned series was to emerge:

Le Mystère de l'Atelier 15 (1957)

Production Company	Les Films Jacqueline Jacoupy
Producer	Jacqueline Jacoupy
Directors	Alain Resnais, André Heinrich
Technical Supervisors	André Vallaud, Georges Smagghe
Camera Operators	Ghislain Cloquet, Sacha Vierny
Editor	Anne Sarraute
Music	Pierre Barbaud
Musical Director	Georges Delerue
Sound	Studio Marignan
Commentary	Chris Marker
Narrator	Jean-Pierre Grenier

'With the collaboration of': Chris Marker, Yves Peneau, Jean Brugot, Fernand Marzelle, Claude Joudioux, André Schlotter, Fearless Fosdick, Elisabeth Seibel.
Running time, 18 mins.
Distributors: Consortium/Pathé-Cinéma (France)

Le Chant du Styrène (1958)

Production Company	La Société Pechiney
Producer	Pierre Braunberger
Director	Alain Resnais

Director of Photography	Sacha Vierny (Dyaliscope)
Colour Process	Eastman Colour
Editor	Alain Resnais
Music	Pierre Barbaud
Musical Director	Georges Delerue
Commentary	Raymond Queneau
Narrator	Pierre Dux

Running time, 19 mins.

Acknowledgements

Grateful thanks for stills are due to:
Compton-Cameo/Sebricon (*L'Année Dernière à Marienbad*); Contemporary Films (*L'Immortelle*); Gala Film Distributors (*Hiroshima Mon Amour, La Guerre est Finie*); United Artists (*Muriel*); Como Film (*Trans-Europ Express*); Films Raoul Ploquin (*La Musica*); Parc Films (*Je t'aime, Je t'aime*); Sofracima (*Le Coup de Grâce*).
To Unifrance Film.
To Liliane de Kermadec for the cover picture from *Muriel* and the production still.
To Cedric Pheasant for frame stills from *La Guerre est Finie, Hiroshima Mon Amour, Muriel, Guernica, Van Gogh*.
To Philip Strick for *Guernica* and *Van Gogh* sequences.

Je t'aime, Je t'aime: Carla Marlier →